JEWS
AGAINST
THEMSELVES

JEWS AGAINST THEMSELVES

Edward Alexander

Transaction Publishers

New Brunswick (U.S.A.) and London (U.K.)

Library of Congress Catalog Number: 2014034988
ISBN: 978-1-4128-5603-4 (cloth); 978-1-4128-5682-9 (paper)
Printed in the United States of America

Library of Congress Cataloging-in-Publication Data

Alexander, Edward, author.
Jews against themselves / Edward Alexander.
    pages cm
  ISBN 978-1-4128-5603-4
    1. Israel and the diaspora. 2. Jews--United States--Attitudes toward Israel. 3. Holocaust, Jewish (1939-1945)--Influence. 4. Jews--United States--Intellectual life. 5. Arab-Israeli conflict--Foreign public opinion, American. 6. Public opinion--United States. 7. Israel--Foreign public opinion, American. I. Title.
DS132.A44 2015
305.892'4--dc23

                                                        2014034988

In Memoriam

Sadie and Harry Alexander

Sadie's Last Apartment

here we are asea
in spice jars of hearing aid batteries
mothballs nestled like spider eggs among the canned goods
enough spools of colored thread to bandolier a tailors' brigade
the maker's mark on the dinner plates saved for best
isn't Rozenburg but union bug
take care and dry your eyes

with salted fingertips
orbit the rim of a sturdy dish and try to make it sing
like a glass harmonica but what rings out
is a full-throated stoneware chorus
a brother/sisterhood of potters
kicking the wheel of memory
take care and tune your ear to it

listen for the thud and wet shatter
of a milk bottle your grandfather's hand deployed
to keep his friend from the wrong side of the picket line
the same hand
that proffered chocolate coins and silver dollars
and bade you
take these tokens for the long ride home

the tunnel oscillates light and shadow
the passing trains of past and present chunter through
black and gold pulsate a syncopated tick and hum
in the scissoring interstices

on the hypnotic dial of Harry's watch
like the third rail of every untold story
take care and keep your distance

but come close now for the journey back
three brothers in the stifling hold of the Gothland
names and ages shifting like silt on the ocean floor
one will meet this dark-haired whipsmart girl
who darts undaunted across a bustling avenue
they will dance the Charleston on a tenement roof
take care to remember:
the body is a strict boss but the spirit doesn't punch the clock

©Rebecca Alexander 9-7-2014

Contents

"Antisemitism directed at oneself was an original Jewish creation. I don't know of any other nation so flooded with self-criticism. Even after the Holocaust . . . harsh comments were made by prominent Jews against the victims. . . . The Jewish ability to internalize any critical and condemnatory remark and castigate themselves is one of the marvels of human nature. . . . Day and night . . . that feeling produces dread, sensitivity, self-criticism and sometimes self-destruction."

—Aharon Appelfeld (*New York Times Book Review*, February 28, 1988)

Acknowledgments

For help and suggestions of various kinds, I am grateful to David Alexander, Rebecca Alexander, Jerold Auerbach, Paul Bogdanor, Maier Deshell (z"l), Rivkah Fishman, Jonathan Imber, Rob Jacobs, Laurie Josephs, Ruth King, Neal Kozodoy, Jonathan Marks, Andrew McIntosh, Louis Offen, Cynthia Ozick, Nikolai Popov, Walter Reich, Alvin Rosenfeld, Gabriel Schoenfeld, Todd Warnick, Douglas Wertheimer.

I am grateful to the following journals for permission to reprint essays, in whole or in part.

Algemeiner
"Choose Your Side: The New York Times or Judaism," March 18, 2013.
"Jews Against Themselves," May 14, 2014.

Chicago Jewish Star
"Ashamed Jews: *The Finkler Question*," December 10, 2010.

Commentary Magazine
"Liberalism and Zionism," February 1986.
"Noam Chomsky and Holocaust Denial," November 1993.
"Disraeli and Marx," June 1994, October 1996.

Jewish Press
"Jewish Israel-Haters Convert Their Dead Grandmothers: A New Mormonism?," January 28, 2011.

Society (A Springer Periodical)
"Past and Present," January/February 2013.

The Weekly Standard
"America's Academic Boycotters," December 2013.
"The Campus Is Conquered . . . ," November 10, 2014.

Introduction

I

The New Apostasy, in Historical Perspective

This book is about the new forms taken by Jewish apostasy in an age when Jewish existence is threatened more starkly and immediately than at any time since the Nazi war against the Jews, waged from 1933 to 1945. The enormity of this apostasy cannot be measured without identifying what and whom its practitioners embrace. In the Middle East, Israel is surrounded by enemies who, both of their own volition and as agents of the genocidal Iranian regime, are not merely bent on Israel's destruction but deem it their own *raison d'être*, being far less interested in building up their own societies than in destroying the society of their neighbor. Appeasement of Iran itself, despite its undisguised, relentless drive to obtain nuclear weapons, and its constant reiteration of the goal of obliterating Israel, is now the order of the day even in the United States and the United Kingdom.

Nor does Europe, which not very long ago destroyed its own civilization in the process of erasing its Jewish population, present a happier scene. Raul Hilberg once encapsulated the history of Europe's treatment of its Jewish minority as follows: "The missionaries of Christianity had said in effect: You have no right to live among us as Jews. The secular rulers who followed had proclaimed: You have no right to live among us. The German Nazis at last decreed: You have no right to live."[1] He also called it "a cyclical trend," meaning a phenomenon that recurs. The "dark continent" of Europe appears to have recommenced the cycle. For several years now, primarily in Germany but also in other European countries, the campaigns against circumcision ("bodily mutilation" or "violation of the rights of children") and kosher slaughter ("cruelty to animals") have been gaining ever-wider support, and this among people who show no concern whatever about tonsillectomy or the way in which lobsters are killed. The banning of circumcision and of kashrut would indeed make it impossible for most Jews (perhaps even those who felt the need to return to a continent whose rivers once flowed with Jewish blood) to live "as Jews" in Poland or Germany or France. As if this were not enough to threaten the continuation of Jewish life in Europe, there is the little matter of the old continent's inability to cope with the Israelophobia and generalized Jew-hatred of its rapidly multiplying and increasingly violent Muslim minority except by blaming its woes on its (peaceful) Jewish minority, especially those Jews who assert Israel's "right to exist," and do so in countries that not so long ago questioned Jews' "right to live."

Almost as menacing as the physical threat to Jewish existence posed by genocidally inclined Persians and Arabs and Muslim sympathizers beyond measure is the new climate of opinion, succinctly described by David Nirenberg: "We live in an age in which millions of people are exposed daily to some variant of the argument that the challenges of the world they live in are best explained in terms of 'Israel.'"[2]

In the summer of 2014, Israel's self-defense against thousands of Hamas bombardments of its cities from the southern border and north to Haifa brought tens of thousands of violent, often murderous, anti-Jewish rioters into the streets of London, Belfast, Paris, Oslo, Amsterdam, Antwerp, and Berlin. This led to desperate warnings from several heads of government that Europeans should remember how their destruction of European Jewish civilization in World War II had also set their own civilization ablaze. During July 2014 there were larger demonstrations in support of Hamas in European cities than in any Arab capital. The European mob that used to chant "*Mort aux Juifs*" and "*Juden Raus*" was now delivering the same message in a different linguistic and cultural medium: "*Khaybar, Khaybar ya-Yahud, jaish Mohammad saya'ud*" (Mohammad is coming back [to slaughter and enslave Jews] as he did in the Battle of Khaybar). Danes were shocked to see the flag of this Islamist version of Nazism flying, with approval of the Bishop of Copenhagen, from the Protestant Stephan's Church in Copenhagen.

French Jewry, the largest Jewish community in the European Union, is now rapidly shrinking as a result of the country's intense and frequently violent antisemitism,* emanating not only from Muslim "activists," but from all parts of the political spectrum in the land of "Liberty, Equality, Fraternity—or Death." Michel Gurfinkiel, writing in the *Jewish Chronicle* (June 27, 2014), predicted French Jewry's rapid decline, by the end of 2014, from half a million to 400,000. French Jewish immigration to Israel now approaches 6,000 to 7,000 annually, and emigration to other countries is also rising rapidly. In recent years French-born jihadists have committed gruesome murders of Jews in Toulouse and Brussels; in the summer of 2014, they organized attacks on synagogues in a French version of *Kristallnacht*. And as always, just as surely as night follows day, France's appeasement of its resident antisemites threatens its own existence as well as that of its 2000-year old Jewish community. In early December 2014, Roger Cukierman, longtime president of CRIF, French Jewry's representative body, predicted that "Jews will leave in large numbers and France will fall into the hands of either Shari'a Law or the National Front."

Today's French mob is made up of two sectors: Muslims who declare that "the struggle against the Jews is a sacred duty, even if they leave Greater Syria, until they leave the planet Earth and their property goes to Muslims"[3]; and Frenchmen who believe that "If Israel did not exist, peace and justice would reign in the Middle East." These Frenchmen are the grandchildren of the ones who used to say that "If *Jews* did not exist, there would be no antisemitism."

But the example of France demonstrates that *Jewish* abandonment of Israel—the subject of this book—is not an inevitable result of anti-semitism. Compared with England or Germany, France has relatively few Jews who have turned on Israel and sided with its enemies. Does the daily threat of violence by antisemites help to concentrate the mind? In Germany, relatively free until recently of anti-Jewish violence, the organized Jewish community has seen fit to lavish honors upon Judith Butler, one of the most fanatical Jewish Israel-haters in the world. In September 2012 she was invited by the Berlin Jewish Museum to ride her hobbyhorse—the need to boycott Israel—in public. In 2013 the museum invited Brian Klug, in 2014 Antony Lerman, anti-Zionist Jews whose loathing of Israel rivals Butler's. The museum's witless directors have apparently forgotten that the Nazi boycott of Jewish stores in 1933 was conceived in Berlin. (It is also safe to assume that German Jews influenced the selection of Butler for the Theodor Adorno Prize.)

The essays in this book deal with Jewish apostates of a new kind, defined by Cynthia Ozick in a startling essay of 2008 entitled "Apostasy, Then and Now":

> How, then, should we look at this word *apostate* today? That it has mostly fallen into disuse we know; yet its freight has been put to many uses, especially under the noose of successive creedal tyrannies. Inevitably . . . it returns us to the theme of defamation. The apostate is one who defames—if not his origins explicitly, then his living counterparts, the people to whom he was born. . . . The notion of

apostasy still holds. But its meaning has been curiously reversed. The Nicholas Donins and Pablo Christianis of ages past ran to abandon their Jewish ties even as they subverted them. The Nicholas Donins and Pablo Christianis of our own time run to embrace their Jewish ties even as they besmirch them. So it is as self-declared Jews, as loyal and honorable Jews, as Jews in the line of the prophets . . . that we nowadays hear arguments against the survival, or the necessity, or the legitimacy, of the state of Israel.[4]

Ozick did not, however, think it necessary to explain in detail why this appropriation of the long robes and long faces of biblical prophets is fraudulent. The biblical prophets excoriated Jerusalem not because they hated and wished to destroy it, but because they loved it and wished to preserve it; they did not set themselves apart from Israel's fate or rejoice in its suffering. A true prophet, as the great Israeli scholar Shmaryahu Talmon used to insist, would consider himself successful only if his "predictions" proved wrong.

Customarily, when we use the term "apostasy," we think not of biblical rebels against Mosaic authority like Korach and his sons—who are swallowed up by a selective earthquake as punishment for their mutiny—but of medieval Jews, especially in Spain and France, who converted to Christianity and then outdid the "old" Christians in their zeal to prosecute and persecute their former coreligionists. The Jewish apostate was especially useful to his new church if he was learned and could read Jewish texts, or had himself been a practitioner of what Christians deemed Jewish treachery, and therefore knew it from the inside. Moreover, according to Jewish law (*halacha*) itself, he was *still* a Jew despite having foresworn his old loyalty and identity, and so brought a powerful authenticity and reliability to his slanderous revelations about Jews. (Would a Jew lie, for example, in telling churchmen that unconverted Jewish males menstruated?)

In Ruth Wisse's *Jews and Power* (2007), a short but ambitious book about the Jews' problematic relation to power from 70 CE through the calamitous Oslo accords, the great set piece is a description of the "disputation" of 1263 in Barcelona, sponsored by the king himself, between the Jewish apostate Pablo (Paul) Christiani, who cooked up the scheme, and Rabbi Moses ben Nachman (Nachmanides), the foremost Talmudic scholar of his time. The combatants were to consider the rival claims of Judaism and Christianity to the truth, and to do so exclusively by reference to *Jewish* sources. Not only was Nachmanides prohibited from attacking—as the other side did abundantly—the "lies" of his opponent's religion, and restricted to proving that rabbinic sources did *not* bear witness to Christian truth; he did not, indeed could not, flaunt the political advantage that his opponent did. At the center of their dispute was the reality of power, the contrast between power and powerlessness. The failure of Jews to maintain their sovereignty, argued Christiani, confirmed the failure of their religion. Nachmanides responded by arguing that the "scepter" argument applied only to the tribe of Judah, and not to the entire people of Israel: the scepter, he asserted, had not been removed from Judah, but only suspended—a day might yet come when Jewish power would exceed that of the Christian church.

Nachmanides, it should be noted, did not think Jewish powerlessness a virtue or romanticize and glorify it, as have both humane non-Zionists like Irving Howe (who celebrated Yiddish culture and literature because they embodied "the virtue of powerlessness, the power of helplessness") and also fierce anti-Zionists like Marc Ellis and Daniel Boyarin. These two devotees of the "sissy" school of contemporary Jewish thinkers believe that the moral center of Jewish history is a celebration of the renunciation of national interest, as if that were the only criterion of a just politics; they believe it a virtue in Jews never to have picked up the gun or the knife, as if a man unable to eat should be praised for his ability to fast.

If anyone doubted Pablo's argument about the existing balance of power, the officers of the Dominican inquisition (Dominicans, of whom Pablo was now one, were generally the most intensely anti-Jewish order) were palpably present in the courtroom to reinforce it. Indeed, despite the king's prior assurance of immunity from punishment, Nachmanides was charged with blasphemy and expelled from Spain. In other words, the disputation was as much a trial as a debate. In *Operation Shylock* (1993) Philip Roth wrote that "In the modern world, the Jew has perpetually been on trial; still *today* the Jew is on trial, in the person of the Israeli—and this modern trial of the Jew, this trial which never ends, begins with the trial of Shylock." But he ought to have begun with these medieval debates.

These disputations, it is important to remember, pitted one Jew against another. Conversos were still, according to Jewish law (and also, in many instances, Catholic skepticism about the sincerity of their conversion), Jews; but they were Jews who, at least officially, had seen and embraced the truth, whereas Nachmanides was a Jew still shrouded in darkness.

In that sense, if no other, today's debates, at the Oxford Union or on the BBC, pit Jew against Jew in the medieval scenario. They are designed like those Soviet show-trials that used members of the *Yevsektsia*, the "Jew-section," Communists of Jewish descent, to indict other Jews. The astute English writer Paul Bogdanor has observed that "in the UK today, every Jew, no matter how apolitical or assimilated, has to identify himself either as an enemy of Israel (a 'good Jew' to be showered with plaudits) or a defender of Israel (a 'bad Jew' to be vilified and boycotted)."

In America, unlike England, popular (and also congressional) sympathy for Israel is considerable, and so the Jewish apostate must pretend to put *himself* on trial, conduct a dialogue of his mind with itself, and, eventually finding himself innocent, defame his fellow Jews for supporting Zionism. Thus the aforementioned Ellis, invited some years ago (when he was professor of American and Jewish Studies at Baylor University) by the Union Theological Seminary to address this Christian group on Yom Kippur—the holiest day of the Jewish year—chose to make "public confession" of the sins of (other) Jews. Standing before an audience of learned Protestants on the day when all Jews are being judged by the Almighty, he attacked them, and especially their rabbis, for confessing their sins in synagogues throughout the country. And why? Because they neglected to confess their greatest, overarching sin, which is: their support of Israel. (How Ellis knows what goes on in synagogues on a day that he spends at a Protestant seminary is not made clear.) Never bashful about hectoring others for *their* sins, Ellis upbraids his Christian audience for not doing more abundantly that which they already do—or so one might have thought when many of them are political progressives and members of Presbyterian Church (U.S.A.)—quite adequately: depicting Israel as blacker than Gai-Hinnom and the pit of hell. He singled out for special blame those rabbis who were "enforcing a silence on Christians who want to speak publicly" about how terrible the state of Israel is. As several of the essays in this book point out, the complaint about "silencing all criticism of Israel" is a standard feature of nearly every single piece of bombast out of the mouths of modern Jewish apostates. (Ellis's allegation that Jews in synagogues may be supportive of Israel is also, of course, the rationale invoked by the Paris mob for setting them ablaze.)

I have not attempted a systematic taxonomy of all the species of Jews arrayed under the genus "enemies of Israel," a monumental task that would require an encyclopedia to include the following: Jewish progressives against Israel; Jewish queers against Israel; *Haredim* against Israel; Holocaust survivors against Israel; children of Holocaust survivors against Israel; Jewish Voice for Peace; grandchildren of Holocaust survivors against Israel; survivors of the Warsaw Ghetto against Israel; J Street; Jewish postmodernists against Israel; Jewish Berkeley professors against Israel; post-Zionists against Israel; Jewish members of MESA (Middle East Studies Association) against Israel; Jews for Boycotting Israeli Goods (JBIG, also called, seasonally, London's Jewish Christmas carolers against Israel); and so on and on, *ad infinitum, ad nauseam.* Despite this, there will always be readers who express astonishment that there *are* Jews who question the Jewish right to live as a natural right, or hate Israel and are ashamed to have a state. Surely they are as rare as singing mice or card-playing pigs? Alas, no.

There is also the species called "Israelis against themselves." To them I devote an entire chapter, written with conviction but also hesitation, regret, and wonderment. Most of them continue to live in Israel; some have lost children in Israel's wars. That is to say, they still belong to a community of faith, which chooses to bear a constant burden of peril out of belief that if the Jewish people does not survive in the land of Israel it has no future. And yet . . .

We may conclude, then, that there are important differences between Pablo Christiani or Abner of Burgos of medieval Europe and Marc Ellis or Daniel Boyarin of modern America. Nevertheless we may say of those Jews who have, over the centuries, defamed, abandoned, and harmed their own people: *"Plus ça change, plus c'est la même chose."* The broadest definition of their sin, and one that does not even mention conversion to Christianity or Islam, was given back in the Middle Ages, by none other than Maimonides (1135–1204), and it still holds:

> One who separates himself from the community, even if he does not commit a transgression but only holds aloof from the congregation of Israel, does not fulfill religious precepts in common with his people, shows himself indifferent when they are in distress, does not observe their fasts, but goes his own way, as if he were one of the gentiles and did not belong to the Jewish people—such a person has no share in the world to come.
>
> —Maimonides, *Laws of Repentance,* iii

II

The order in which the essays of this book appear is not in strict chronological accord with the order in which they were first published, but most of the earliest published ones, dealing more with ideas than with events, come early in the book, and most of the recently published ones, centered on events, come in the latter half. Original dates of publication of the essays are given in parentheses below their titles.

I begin with consideration of the dominant form of apostasy in nineteenth-century Europe, which has come to be called "Jewish self-hatred." I move from that to the perverse ways in which the kind of Jew whom Maimonides accuses of "going his own way" and abandoning his people "when they are in distress" has reacted (or failed to react) to the two events of biblical magnitude that have enveloped modern Jewry: the destruction of European Jewry and the founding of the state of Israel. In the last segment of the book, I have succumbed to the parochialism of the contemporary by including three essays about the role played by Jews in the BDS movement to expel Israel from the family of nations, and one about the need for American Jews to decide whether they are going to judge Judaism by the standards of the *New York Times* or the *New York Times* by the standards of Judaism.

I have resisted the temptation (offered by the wisdom of hindsight) to update and "correct" the older essays, hoping instead to get some credit for a bit of prescience by leaving them intact. I might, for example, in my discussion of the intellectual background of the Oslo Accords, have mentioned that one result of those accords, and the relentless emphasis by their Israeli supporters on the irrelevance of land to security, is evident even as I write (summer 2014) in the ability of Hamas to fire its rockets into every corner of Israel. I might also have speculated on what ISIS would now be doing to Israel had Israel withdrawn from the Golan Heights. But I have not.

Preserving the essays in their original form means that certain nodal points or touchstones will be repeated, in the same way that Matthew Arnold keeps returning, in his essays, like a patient schoolmaster, to certain familiar landmarks like "sweetness and light," "doing as one likes," "the best that is known and thought and felt in the world." If verbal recurrence sometimes annoys, it more frequently serves to drive home a crucial point.

III

About the Author (by the Author)

My most vivid and satisfying memory of growing up in the Brownsville section of Brooklyn dates from May 1948, when I was eleven and a half years old. Jackie Robinson, who then lived adjacent to my high school, was beginning the second year of his brilliant career with the Dodgers, and for me and most of my friends, he was the greatest man in the world. Coming a close second to Robinson in our esteem was David Ben-Gurion, whose declaration that month that the Jews, like other peoples, now had a state of their own, ignited dancing in the streets. These two heroic figures came together for me almost magically when I heard Robinson address a block party (either on Amboy Street or the adjacent Hopkinson Avenue) to celebrate Israel's independence. I consider myself lucky never to have been disillusioned about what my parents taught me: that both men symbolized the belated righting of ancient historical wrongs, that Robinson was indeed a uniquely courageous figure and that the birth of Israel just a few years after the destruction of European Jewry was one of the greatest affirmations of life ever made by a martyred people, indeed what Ruth Wisse would later call the most hopeful sign for humanity since the dove came back to Noah with an olive leaf after the primeval flood.

Elsewhere in this book the reader will come upon Jewish memoirists who regret that their 1940s interest in baseball was a distraction from Jewish concerns, but my experience was the opposite. The linkage between Jewish and Negro rebirth was reinforced in my Hebrew school (providentially located on 500 Herzl Street) by Principal Rabbi Z. Harry Gutstein's system of rewards for boys who could recite the Shema from memory or show mastery of Hebrew conjugations: good work was rewarded with "points" that could lead to tickets to Dodger games. Some years later I also came to understand that one reason why Brooklyn (and not Boston or Philadelphia or St. Louis) became the site for the experiment in integrating baseball was precisely its large Jewish population and its sense of brotherhood with the Negro. "Bliss was it in that dawn to be alive, and to be young was very heaven."

But, like Wordsworth, I was to be disillusioned—not by Israel, which has had to mobilize for, and survive, sixty-six years of relentless military and ideological onslaught, such as no other nation has endured (or could endure)—but by Jews of the "progressive" persuasion. They have not only failed to mobilize their intellectual resources on behalf of a constantly besieged country, but have abandoned it to, where they have not actually joined, its enemies, and become "Jews against themselves." Who among us could have imagined that liberalism, which so many modern Jews have adopted as their *raison d'être*, would itself become dogmatic, would acquire a craving for forbidden fruit (and its legalization), and—this above all—would abandon the Jews, and turn against Zionism and the state of Israel? Ian Buruma did not exaggerate when he wrote, over a decade ago, in the *New York Times Magazine*, that "the Palestinian cause has become the universal litmus of liberal credentials." (To readers of that newspaper, of course, this must have seemed the most banal of commonplaces.) Which of us youngsters was even aware of Zionism's emphasis upon "negation of the Diaspora" lest the Diaspora negate Zionism? Indeed, how many *adult* Jews in 1948 could have imagined that the Holocaust would cast its specter of blood and shame over the Jews well into the next century, that its "lesson" would be not "Never again," but—for the victims—"It happened once, it can happen again" and for the perpetrators—"We did it once, we can do it again."

Notes

*   I use the spelling "antisemitism" (not "anti-Semitism") because there is no such thing as a "Semitism" to which Jew-haters are opposed.
     The term was coined in the 1870s in Europe by people looking for a euphemistic, pseudo-scientific term for the old-fashioned "Jew-hatred," which had begun to sound nasty. Antisemites do not hate Semites; they hate Jews. Getting rid of that hyphen (and the capital letter) doesn't entirely solve the problem, but it helps to prevent obfuscation.

1.   *The Destruction of the European Jews* (Chicago: Quadrangle Books, 1961), 3–4.
2.   David Nirenberg, *Anti-Judaism: The Western Tradition* (New York: Norton, 2013), 471.
3.   Pierre-Andre Taguieff, *Rising from the Muck: The New Anti-Semitism in Europe* (Chicago: Ivan R. Dee, 2004), 27.
4.   Cynthia Ozick, "Apostasy, Then and Now," in *Israel's Jewish Defamers* (Boston: Camera, 2008). As recently as 1987 Todd Endelman published a collection of essays by various scholars entitled *Modern Jewish Apostasy* (New York: Holmes and Meier). None of them mentions the anti-Zionists discussed in this book.

1

Jewish Self-Hatred (1986)

Rare is the critique of Israel's Jewish defamers that does not disparage them as "self-haters" or reject that time-dishonored label as grotesquely unsuited to people who seem rather to suffer from a self-love of prodigious proportions. Both schools of criticism might benefit from reconsidering the origins of this peculiarly Jewish phenomenon.

It is often alleged that Jews expend too much time, energy, and ingenuity on the subject of antisemitism, which is a Gentile problem or "sickness," not a Jewish one. Yet it is undeniable that "self-hating" Jews have made such large contributions to the ideology and politics of antisemitism that it may fairly be called a product (perhaps the only genuine one) of the "Judeo-Christian tradition." Before Pope Gregory IX ordered the Talmud to be seized, examined, and publicly burnt in Paris and Rome, he was presented in 1239 with a detailed analysis of the manifold evils of the Jews' religious books from the Dominican brother Nicholas Donin, a Jewish convert possessed of the "special" knowledge of these poisonous books that only a Jew could have. In the sixteenth century Martin Luther's seemingly innovative program of burning synagogues, destroying Jewish homes, and confiscating the Talmud and all other Hebrew books was in fact derived from the proposals of Johannes (formerly Josef) Pfefferkorn, the Jewish convert who, years earlier, had exhorted his German countrymen to "drive the old Jews out like dirty dogs and baptize the young children" and "take their goods and give them to those to whom they belong." Christians appear to have invented, all on their own, the belief in Jewish male menstruation, but doubters among them received assurance from Jewish converts such as Franco de Piacenza, who in 1630 revealed to the world the shameful secret that Jewish males of the lost tribe of Simeon menstruated four days a year. The belief of Martin Luther and his acolytes that Yiddish was the language of thieves

1

and constituted a sin against the German tongue was actively supported by many Jews from his own time through that of Moses Mendelssohn, who warned that Yiddish degraded culture.

The fruitful interaction between Christian antisemites and Jewish self-haters, a process in which it is difficult to disentangle cause from effect, continued after the Enlightenment and is as real and living today as ever it was. The German antisemites who said that Heine smelled—devilish Jews have not only the horns, tail, beard, and sexuality, but also the smell, of the goat—found confirmation of their views in Heine's own depiction of the Polish Jew with "his lousy beard, with his garlic breath, and his bad German." Socialist antisemites heard from the converted Jew Karl Marx the assertion that capitalism is nothing other than the Talmud written in the real language of the Jews, which is neither Hebrew nor Yiddish, but "haggling." Feminist antisemites could find in the same "Jewish" source the insistence that "in the Jewish religion . . . woman is bartered." Perhaps the ultimate example of the "German-Jewish symbiosis" is the relation between attacks by such Jewish self-haters as Karl Kraus upon Jewish perversions of the pure German tongue and Hitler's demand that works written by Jews in German be labeled translations.

This pattern whereby "in inexorable dialectic, each self-hating text generates new anti-Jewish texts" is the subject of Sander Gilman's *Jewish Self-Hatred: Anti-Semitism and the Hidden Language of the Jew*. Gilman set himself to examine "how Jews see the dominant society seeing them and how they project their anxiety about this manner of being seen onto other Jews as a means of externalizing their own status anxiety."[1] Gilman claims that the form of self-abnegation called self-hatred has existed throughout Jewish history, and that it is a term interchangeable with "Jewish anti-Semitism." His working definition of the Jew is "one perceived and treated as a Jew," and, following Sartre, he views the Jews' sense of their identity as always and only "reactive" to groups labeling them as "Other." He works from the assumption, for which he provides much evidence, that "Otherness" and self-hatred are best examined in language because the dominant or "reference" groups in societies where Jews have lived have always alleged that Jews cannot possess the language of their environment because they have a hidden language of their own. For this reason he has undertaken to analyze the work of Jews, from the Middle Ages to the present day, who have relied upon writing and language for their status in society. The texts he selects for study, at least prior to the Holocaust, are mainly German, and he takes for granted the German-centered view of Jewish history that has been called into question by such Jewish historians as Todd Endelman.

The centrality of fulminations against the Jews' hidden language in the forms of self-hatred makes for a continuity that is uncanny in its lunatic persistence in Jewish intellectual history. In the Middle Ages, Gilman notes, Hebrew was the magical language *par excellence*, and one reason why a charlatan like Pfefferkorn could hypnotize audiences for hours "while he expounded on topics about which he knew nothing" was that he knew some of that mysterious tongue. But since Hebrew was the language of the Scripture, a Jew could not really command it until he became a Christian. Some Jew-haters therefore claimed that the hidden language of the Jews was not Hebrew at all, but the lie. Luther denied to all Jews, including converts, any "true" knowledge of Hebrew beyond the alphabet. Even the great nineteenth-century scholar Ernest Renan argued that Hebrew was only natural to the Jews when they used it to express the "monotheism of the desert."

When accusations against the hidden language of the Jews made Yiddish rather than Hebrew the target, Jewish self-haters responded by saying that not they but their backward cousins from the east were inarticulate, barbarous, corrupt. Like the converts of earlier centuries, the German-Jewish intellectuals of the Enlightenment tried to deal with their own self-doubt and insecurity by deflecting the charges made against Jews in general onto other Jews: Yiddish speakers. Thus Mendelssohn referred to Yiddish translations of the Bible as written in "a language of stammerers, corrupt and deformed, repulsive to those who are able to speak in correct and orderly manner" (102).

Jewish intellectual self-hatred often prompted flight as well as denunciation, but since the flight was from oneself, it could be an arduous, frustrating journey. Gilman is at his best in describing the struggle for a truly German linguistic identity by such talented self-haters as Borne, Heine, and Marx. Ludwig Borne (Judah Low Baruch before he became a Lutheran) flees from his religion, from his native Yiddish language, and then finds, to his discomfiture, that he is still seen as a Jew because "he bears the stigma of the new language of the Jews, not Yiddish but irony" (162). He then espouses the antisemitic views of the 1819 "HepHep" rioters and re-creates himself as the liberal journalist excoriating the bad, moneyed Jews—only to find that "liberal journalist" has now become synonymous with "Jew" (154, 166).

Baruch-Borne served as a model for Johann Christian Heinrich Heine, who before his baptism was Harry Heine. No sooner had he

converted than he condemned his friend Eduard Gans for committing the "unforgivable felony"—namely, converting. Subsequently, he
too found that no matter where he fled, he was confronted by himself. His Lutheran "ticket of admission" to European culture proved
worthless: he was "now hated by Christian and Jew alike," "sorry that
I permitted myself to be baptized," and condemned to endless suffering by "that never removable Jew" that he would be no matter what
discourse he used (176–81). Whereas Borne and Heine projected all
their own faults onto their Jewish identity, Karl Marx, converted at
age six, found himself perceived as a Jew although his Jewish identity
was virtually nonexistent, although he tried to make his life into the
antithesis of the image of the Jew, and although he outdid most of
his contemporaries in pouring scorn and hatred on the Jews. The
worst thing Marx could think to say of the German-Christian state
was that it was "Jewish" in its corrupt art and language. In a curious
throwback to the medieval view of apostates, Marx held that the
only good Jew was the exJew (200). But since the Jews lacked free
will, they could never alter their essence and so inevitably poisoned
their environment. With surgical precision and deftness, Gilman
reveals how Marx, in the tradition of Jewish antisemites since the
Middle Ages, imputes to Jews other than himself false language,
bad manners, and sexual aggressiveness. Of the "Jewish nigger"
Ferdinand Lassalle (himself a Jewish antisemite of formidable de-
rangement), Marx writes, "Always this constant babble with the
falsely excited voice, the unaesthetic, demonstrative gestures, . . .
and also the uncultivated eating and the horny lust of this 'idealist.' . . .
As his skull shape and hair prove, he is a descendant of those Blacks
who accompanied Moses on the exodus from Egypt. . . . Now this
combination of Jewishness and Germanness upon the Black basic
substance must bring forth a strange product. The pushiness of this
fellow is also nigger-like" (206). Of course it came as a shattering
disappointment to Marx when his new, "non-Jewish" language of
revolution was labeled Jewish. As Gilman shrewdly says of the Vien-
nese Jewish antisemite Arthur Trebitsch, who believed himself to be
pierced by electromagnetic rays beamed by the Jewish conspiracy,
"Since the Jews that he feared were hidden within him, everywhere
that he fled he felt himself pursued" (249).

Having established, with a thoroughness of scholarship and cogency
of argument that cannot fail to evoke admiration, the dominant pattern of Jewish self-hatred since the Middle Ages, Gilman is reluctant

to part with it. That is one reason why, when he comes to deal with western Jews who, from the late nineteenth century onward, appear to be reversing the old pattern of self-hatred by aspiring toward a positive image of the unassimilated, unenlightened eastern Jew, Gilman insists that the "positive stereotype" of the *Ostjude* is itself—whether expressed by Buber or Kafka or Hans Kohn—an expression of selfdoubt and self-hatred (285–86). Thus the critics of self-hatred are themselves held to be guilty of self-hatred. They are merely assigning a positive value to the antisemites' old images of Jewish uniqueness by rejecting self-hatred as "sick" (a term Gilman does not allow) and inventing a "healthy" Jew who exists only "in the never-never land of myth" (300), a term Gilman uses in the crude sense of denial of "reality"). Having devoted three hundred pages to a frightful nosology of the varieties of self-hatred, he turns with ferocity upon those who indulge in "the polemic attached to the idea of selfhatred as the pathological underpinning of the 'bad' Jew," and says *tu quoque*.

The last quarter of this book, despite many fine things in it, is vitiated by a philosophical agnosticism that will not distinguish between the contending claims to Jewishness of Karl Kraus and Theodor Herzl, or Haskalah and Hasidism, or Cynthia Ozick and Anne Roiphe, or a German-style *Gymnasium* and "'Jewish' structures such as the *heder*." For Gilman the inner world of the Jews is a vast hall of mirrors, nothing in itself, everything by reflection and reaction. Sometimes, indeed, he writes as if the outer world of the Jews was only "images." He quotes Kafka's vivid description of the Belzer *rebbe* as both dirty and clean, and immediately "translates" this into the "traditional" antisemitic image of the bad Jew and its inverted romanticization in Buber's good Jew. Meanwhile Kafka's insight into the paradox, that precisely those Jews who are fit to see God may be unfit to be seen or touched or smelled by anybody else, is lost.

Gilman's hostility toward those who presume to distinguish between good and bad Jews leads him to resolve the controversy over the true meaning of Anne Frank's diary in favor of Lillian Hellmann rather than Meyer Levin. In the *Diary* Anne Frank wrote, "If we bear all this suffering and if there are still Jews left, when it is over, then Jews . . . will be held up as an example. . . . We can never become just Netherlanders . . . or just representatives of any other country . . . we will always remain Jews." In the Hackett-Hellmann stage version, this was reduced to: "We are not the only people that've had to suffer . . . sometimes one race, sometimes another." The stage version is, not to put too fine a point upon it, a lie;

but Gilman's determination to present Levin as a self-hating Jew obliges him to turn Levin's excoriation of that lie into a mere device for abusing German Jews (such as Hellmann) as corrupt and degenerate.

Gilman concludes his book with a subtle argument about the "closure" on the concept of the self-hating Jew that has been achieved by Philip Roth and other writers mindful of the difference between European and American antisemitism. But he does not suggest that self-hatred is dead, and notes that "one of the most recent forms of Jewish self-hatred is the virulent Jewish opposition to the existence of the State of Israel" (391). In one sense, Gilman's demonstration of the permanence of Jewish self-hatred in the Diaspora converges with a major premise of Zionism. Amos Oz once wrote that "I am a Zionist because I cannot live and have no desire to live like the reflected image of a symbol imprinted in other peoples' imaginations, neither as the symbol of a crafty and diabolic vampire nor as the symbol of a piteous victim to whom one must offer compassion and compensation. That is why there is no place in the world for me other than the country of the Jews."[2]

But it is now becoming clear that self-hatred, like other afflictions of the Jews in exile, has taken up residence in the country of the Jews itself. Ever since the passage in 1975 of the Zionism-racism resolution by the UN (under the stewardship of Kurt Waldheim), countless Israeli intellectuals have doggedly devoted themselves to ferreting out and theatrically deploring evidences of the "racism" of their less western, less enlightened, less progressive countrymen. During the 1982 (Lebanon) war, a whole range of Israelis whom nobody outside of Israel had ever heard of before, from professors to publishers of pornographic newspapers, became instant European celebrities by applying the epithet "Judeo-Nazi" to other Israelis, in precisely the style of "projection" that antisemitic Jews have been practicing since the Middle Ages.

Notes

1. *Jewish Self-Hatred: Anti-Semitism and the Hidden Language of the Jews* (Baltimore: Johns Hopkins University Press, 1986), 11, 15, 47, 67. Subsequent references to this book are given in parentheses in the text.
2. Amos Oz, "Homeland," in *Under the Blazing Light* [in Hebrew] (Tel Aviv: Sifriat Poalim, 1979), 73.

2

Disraeli and Marx: *Stammgenosse?* (1994, 1996)

Although Karl Marx wrote many thousands of words (nearly all vituperative, and many salacious) about Jews, he seems to have mentioned his own Jewish origins only once. In a letter to Lion Philips, a Dutch uncle who founded the Philips Electronics dynasty and was a major source of (capitalist) income to young Marx, he remarks that Benjamin Disraeli is their *Stammgenosse*, that is, of the same stock.[1] Why, one wonders, should the fierce Promethean rebel against established society and Western imperialism claim kinship with the quintessential insider—the traditionalist (and imperialist) Tory politician Disraeli? Although he was willing to grant that Young England, the political movement and parliamentary faction headed by Disraeli, occasionally struck the bourgeoisie "in the very heart's core" by its witty and incisive criticisms, Marx nevertheless dismissed it as a fantastical sentimentalism, with a "total incapacity to comprehend the march of history."[2]

Of course Marx would have known, if not in particular detail, that Disraeli, like himself, came from a Jewish family that had formally abandoned its religious traditions, and might have felt some affinity with him on that account. Their experiences of separation from Judaism have a broad similarity, but are by no means identical.

Although born to Jewish parents, Marx was baptized at age six into the Lutheran faith in the Rhineland city of Trier, whose rabbi was his uncle. Although his Voltairean father had joined the Lutheran church a year earlier (1817), Karl's mother held out against conversion until age thirty-eight, when her father, a rabbi of Nigmejen, Holland, died. For this tardiness as well as other "despised remnants of Judaic practice," Marx remained permanently resentful of her. She was also guilty of

7

remarking, "If only Karell had made Capital instead of writing about it."[3] He openly expressed to Engels his wish that his mother would drop dead, and she complied within a year of his entreaty.

Indeed, Marx wished the same for any relative likely to bequeath money to him and his wife, Jenny, the daughter of a German baron. Marx's treatment of his family and his willingness to sacrifice his wife and children to "the revolution" are likely to remind us of the English novelist George Eliot's advice that "it is sometimes better not to follow great reformers of abuses beyond the threshold of their homes."[4]

Given the fact that, for thousands of admirers as well as detractors, "the Jew Marx" has the fixity of Homeric epithet, it is worth recalling that Marx's Lutheran education was stringent, not perfunctory, and that it had deep and lasting effects upon him. Despite the incessant labeling, from that day to this, of Marx as a Jew, his extant papers contain not so much as a scribble of a Hebrew letter, whereas his style is permeated by the language and even worldview of the Lutheran Bible. "Luther," Marx's biographer Frank Manuel observes, "is one of the few religious leaders Marx ever cited with approval,"[5] and in *Das Kapital* he is invoked as an authority on the economic transformations of sixteenth-century Germany.

Disraeli remarked that "I was not bred among my race and was nourished in great prejudice against them."[6] His grandmother, Sarah Shiprut de Gabay, was a Jewish antisemite so venomous that Disraeli's biographer Stanley Weintraub speculates that she may have provided (via Disraeli's memoir of his father) the germ for George Eliot's feminist antisemite in her "Jewish" novel *Daniel Deronda*, Princess Alcharisi. Disraeli's father, Isaac D'Israeli, was, in Cynthia Ozick's words, "the perfect English man of letters, easily comparable to, in America now [she wrote in 1970], Lionel Trilling."[7] He did have his son circumcised—an occasion Weintraub describes as "the only Judaic rite in which [Ben] would be a central figure"[8]—but thereafter showed himself to be, just as Heinrich Marx was, the loyal disciple of his beloved Voltaire in matters concerning Judaism. In 1813 he was selected to be a warden of his congregation (Bevis Marks); he rejected the honor, but refused to pay the fine of forty pounds imposed on someone who declined such an office. In March 1817, as young Ben was approaching bar mitzvah age, his father responded with alacrity to a Christian friend's suggestion that he have his children baptized into the Church of England, so that they could have the opportunities available to other English children. On July 11, younger brothers Raphael and Jacobus were duly baptized (and transformed into Ralph and James). Ben was reluctant but succumbed on July 31, with his sister Sarah following shortly after. Thus Benjamin Disraeli was a Jew for seven years longer than Karl Marx, who became a little Lutheran at age six. But Disraeli's parents, unlike Marx's, remained unbaptized.

Hannah Arendt once asserted that assimilated (which in the nineteenth century generally meant converted) Jews often became more obsessed with "Jewishness" than Jews who remained loyal to their religion and their people: "The more the fact of Jewish birth lost its religious, national, and social-economic significance, the more obsessive Jewishness became; Jews were obsessed by it as one may be by a physical defect or advantage, and addicted to it as one may be to a vice."[9] There is some evidence for this claim in the parallel careers of Marx and Disraeli.

Marx, perhaps with the help of his revered Martin Luther, became a ferocious Jew-hater. Throughout his career he mocked the "Jewish" character of his rivals for revolutionary leadership in the Communist and working-class movements. Moses Hess was "Moysi the communist rabbi," and Eduard Bernstein "the little Jew Bernstein." His choicest epithets, however, were reserved for Ferdinand Lassalle. "It is now completely clear to me," wrote Marx to Engels, "that, as his cranial formation and hair show, he is a descendant of the Negroes who attached themselves to the march of Moses out of Egypt (assuming his mother or grandmother on the paternal side had not crossed with a nigger). Now this union of Judaism and Germanism with a basic negroid substance must yield a strange product. The pushiness of the fellow is also Nigger-like." Moses Mendelssohn was a "shit-windbag"; Polish Jews were said by Marx to multiply like lice and to be the "filthiest of all races." On a holiday in Ramsgate, he complained that the place "is full of Jews and fleas." Despite the loneliness of that single reference to Disraeli as his Jewish kin, Frank Manuel argues that Marx was at some subconscious level always aware of the profound effects that Jewish antisemitism can have upon Jews. "Self-contempt," Marx wrote in a youthful essay prefiguring his own psychic fate, "is a serpent constantly gnawing at one's breast; it sucks the life-blood out of the heart and mixes it with the venom of the hatred of man and of despair."[10]

Frank Manuel's central idea about Marx, in fact, is that his self-hatred was transformed into a universal rage against the existing order of society and bred a utopian fantasy of redemption. "If to Marx Jews were dirty morally and physically and he was a Jew, his denied origins gnawed at his guts on some level of consciousness throughout his life."[11] If the carbuncles that plagued him were the bodily sign of his self-loathing, his utopian hatred of existing society and uncontrollable rages and vendettas against Jewish rivals were its intellectual and political expressions.

Although this idea seems too broadly stated—it is easier to see Marx's self-deception about his Jewish origin at work in his fatuous dismissal of nationalism and ethnicity as forces in political consciousness than in, say, his theory of surplus value—Manuel makes it seem plausible. He is less convincing in his insistence that Marx, despite his exclusively Lutheran education, his Jewish illiteracy ("there is no evidence that he could spell a Hebrew word"), and his Jew-hatred was, after all, "rabbinic," just like his repudiated ancestors. Apparently, not even the shrewdest and best-informed observers can resist the widespread temptation to draft Marx onto the team of Diaspora All-Stars (whose starting lineup also includes, of course, Freud and Einstein). "For anyone who has read Luther's *The Jews and Their Lies*," says Manuel, "a Jewish Lutheran must appear a monstrous oxymoron. But Western culture has shown a penchant for the most outlandish syncretisms, and young Marx's [graduation] essay bears traces of both religious strains . . . a mixed Judeo-Lutheran rhetoric." But from whence did the Judaic strain come? Did Marx inherit in his genes what Manuel calls "the messianic hope . . . passed on through generations of rabbis among both his father's and his mother's forebears"?[12]

One person who might have thought so was Benjamin Disraeli. Disraeli, despite his youthful conversion to Church of England Christianity, was thought of by friends, colleagues, enemies, and himself as a Jew. The philosemitic Matthew Arnold observed that Lord Beaconsfield [Disraeli] "treat[s] Hellenic things with the scornful negligence natural to a Hebrew." The relentlessly antisemitic, radical magazine *Punch* depicted the Disraeli of 1867 as Fagin, stealing the opposition's bill from its back pocket. Carlyle ranted against Disraeli as "a cursed old Jew, not worth his weight in cold bacon." Balliol's famous classical scholar Benjamin Jowett complained about the nation being run by "a wandering Jew." The poet Coventry Patmore bemoaned 1867 as "The year of the great crime, / When the false English nobles, and their Jew, / By God demented, slew / The trust they stood twice pledged to keep from wrong." The former prime minister Palmerston declared, "We are all dreadfully disgusted at the prospect of having a Jew for our Prime Minister." The future liberal prime minister W. E. Gladstone (who had once been Disraeli's rival in the Tory Party) would allege that Disraeli's long-standing pro-Ottoman sympathies and Russophobia were a function of his Jewish sympathies for coreligionists under Russian rule: "Though he has been baptized, his Jew feelings are the most radical & the most real . . . portion of his profoundly falsified nature."[13]

But was Disraeli in fact a Jew? For some time, his inner world, like his outer, showed little sign of his Jewish "background." When he traveled to the Holy Land as a young man, "of Jewish places of worship he saw nothing," and his glowing description of Jerusalem makes no mention of Jews whatever. Such facts would not surprise those of his critics who have alleged that Disraeli's ideas of Jewishness were never disturbed by any actual knowledge of the subject. Nevertheless, in *The Wondrous Tale of Alroy* (1833), he seemed to propose restoring Jerusalem to the Jews. In 1834 he described *Alroy* as a "celebration of a gorgeous incident in that sacred and romantic people from whom I derive my blood and name." Why, his biographer asks, would Disraeli, at the very beginning of a parliamentary career (and frequently thereafter) in a country that still banned real, unconverted Jews from Parliament, glorify his Jewish origins?[14]

Although the answer given by Disraeli's preeminent modern biographer Weintraub is essentially that, however dishonorable Disraeli's behavior may have been with women (in youth he contemned that fraud called "Love") and finance and the grime of political maneuver, he always behaved honorably and "proudly" toward the Jewish background from which he had been severed by his father, the full explanation remains buried deep within the bizarre mixture of sense and (mostly) nonsense that is Disraeli's theory of "racial Judaism." Starting with the plausible notion that, as a character in *Tancred* says, Jesus "was born a Jew, lived a Jew, and died a Jew" (a statement cautiously trimmed in Disraeli's House of Commons allusion to Judaism as "the religion in the bosom of which my Lord and Saviour was born"), Disraeli, very much a Victorian "Jew for Jesus," goes on to refer to Christianity as "completed Judaism" without even the slightest awareness that he thereby confirms the very Christian assumptions he appears to derogate. His novelistic spokesmen urge Jews to be grateful to Christianity because "half Christendom worships a Jewess, and the other half a Jew," and because the Church perpetuates Jewish beliefs, history, literature, culture, and institutions.[15]

Disraeli's ignorance of Judaism was formidable (he was unaware of the dietary laws, and a clergyman in his employ had to remind him—and was fired for doing so—that the Sabbath of which he was so contemptuous was a Jewish institution). But could he really have been blind to the fact that Christianity's vital energy derives from a powerful myth that casts Jews as the enemies of God who, because they rejected and killed Christ, were superseded by a new people and a new covenant? Typically, he referred to himself as "the blank page between the Old Testament and the New"[16] without being aware that he was using terminology that literate Jews consider calumny.

In one sense, Disraeli shared the very racism or at least race-thinking that led English Jew-haters to attack him. Like them, he viewed the Jews not as a community with a specific religion, nationality, and shared memories and hopes, but as a "race," united by blood and even by a conspiracy to rule the world. In *Tancred* (1847) Sidonia, perhaps the most important of Disraeli's fictional spokesmen, sees crypto-Jews managing affairs everywhere, as professors, ambassadors, generals, cabinet members; he also wonders whether Mozart, Haydn, and Beethoven were Jewish too.[17] In *Lord George Bentinck* (1851) we are told, "The first Jesuits were Jews; that mysterious Russian diplomacy which so alarms Western Europe is organized and principally carried on by Jews . . . men of Jewish race are found at the head of every one of [communist and socialist] groups. The people of God co-operates with atheists; the most skilful accumulators of property ally themselves with communists."[18] In *Endymion*, a novel that Disraeli (with characteristically unflagging energy) wrote just after retiring from politics in 1880, a sympathetic character observes that "Semites now exercise a vast influence over affairs through their smallest though most peculiar family, the Jews."[19]

Hannah Arendt, in perhaps the fiercest attack on Disraeli ever written by a Jew, correctly pointed out that he "produced the entire set of theories about Jewish influence and organization that we usually find in the more vicious forms of antisemitism." He did so, she alleged, "almost automatically," that is to say, as a result of carrying to extreme or radical form what she calls the characteristic superstition of assimilated Jews—namely, that Judaism is nothing more than a fact of birth. "Disraeli, though certainly not the only 'exception Jew' to believe in his own chosenness without believing in Him who chooses and rejects, was the only one who produced a full-blown race doctrine out of this empty concept of a historic mission."[20]

Although Arendt is not able to show that the European antisemites who are her main concern were influenced by so (to them) obscure a source as Disraeli's written work, there is no doubt that some of the most savage attacks on Disraeli by his English contemporaries were provoked by his insistence that "all is race." Perhaps the most shocking of these attacks is that by George Eliot, writing in 1848:

> D'Israeli [sic] is unquestionably an able man, and I always enjoy his tirades against liberal principles as opposed to popular principles—the name by which he distinguishes his own. As to his theory of races, it has not a leg to stand on, and can only be buoyed up by such windy eloquence as—You chubby-faced, squabby-nosed Europeans owe your commerce, your arts, your religion, to the Hebrews,—nay, the Hebrews lead your armies: in proof of which he can tell us that Massena, a second-rate general of Napoleon's, was a Jew, whose real name was Manasseh. . . .The fellowship of race, to which D'Israeli so exultingly refers the munificence of Sidonia, is so evidently an inferior impulse, which must ultimately be superseded, that I wonder even he, Jew as he is, dares to boast of it. My Gentile nature kicks most resolutely against any assumption of superiority in the Jews, and is almost ready to echo Voltaire's vituperation. I bow to the supremacy of Hebrew poetry, but much of their early mythology, and almost all their history, is utterly revolting.[21]

This is the same George Eliot now revered by Jews as a Judeophile and early Zionist, the woman for whom a street is named (deservedly) in each of Israel's three major cities.

A street is also named in Jerusalem for Benjamin Disraeli himself. Just why, one wonders? Is it because he was obsessed with "Jewishness" in his writings? Is it because, despite having been turned into a Christian by his father, he behaved "honorably" in relation to his Jewish ancestry? Is it perhaps because several of his works, such as *Alroy*, can be construed as Zionist in idea or impulse, and he often spoke to friends about his dream of "restoring the Jews to their own land"?[22] Or is it because he played a crucial role in committing England (in 1867) to the democratic dispensation and making it into the only European nation that, almost sixty years after his death, resolutely and effectively opposed Hitler's conquest of the world?

Although Marx does not have any streets named after him in Israel, he has for many decades been widely revered by the Israeli left. Shimon Peres, for example, recalls in his memoir *Battling for Peace* how as a young man he courted his beloved Sonia "by reading to her, sometimes by the light of the moon, selected passages from Marx's *Das Kapital*."[23]

Since one assumes that Marx's heroic stature among Israeli leftists cannot be due to the fact that he brought into the world a tremendous power for evil that led to the murder of millions of people around the globe, it must have something to do with the doctrine of economic determinism that helps them to "understand" the apparently permanent state of siege in which they live. Indeed, Peres's constantly reiterated "Marxist" belief that supplying Israel's Arab adversaries with computers and the other accoutrements of modern economic prosperity would lead to a "new Middle East" in which Israel would become a respected member of the Arab League led to the Oslo Accords of 1993, which in turn led to the catastrophic Oslo War launched by Yasser Arafat in September 2000.

Notes

1. Frank E. Manuel, *A Requiem for Karl Marx* (Cambridge, MA: Harvard University Press, 1995), 19.
2. Stanley Weintraub, *Disraeli: A Biography* (New York: Truman Talley Books/ Dutton, 1993), 208.
3. Manuel, *A Requiem*, 11, 101.
4. *Adam Bede* (1859), pt. 1, chap. 5.
5. Manuel, *A Requiem*, 10.
6. Quoted in Hannah Arendt, *Antisemitism* (New York: Harcourt, Brace, and World, 1951), 70n.
7. "Toward a New Yiddish," in *Art and Ardor* (New York: Alfred A. Knopf, 1983), 167.
8. Weintraub, *Disraeli*, 18.
9. *Antisemitism*, 84.
10. Manuel, *A Requiem*, 188, 210, 195, 15, 16, 11.
11. Ibid., 19.
12. Ibid., 21. Even the usually astute Paul Johnson, fully informed as to the fact of Marx's Jewish illiteracy, declares that "virtually all his work . . . has the hallmark of Talmudic study."-- *Intellectuals* (New York: Harper Perennial, 1990), 53.
13. Introduction to *Literature and Dogma*, ed. R. H. Super (Ann Arbor: University of Michigan Press, 1968), 164; Weintraub, *Disraeli*, 536, 441, 453, 462, 577.
14. Ibid., 105, 113.
15. Ibid., 262, 277, 242, 267.
16. Ibid., xii, 278.
17. Ibid., 308.
18. *Lord George Bentinck* (London, 1851), 497.
19. Weintraub, *Disraeli*, 635.
20. *Antisemitism*, 71, 73.
21. J. W. Cross, *Life of George Eliot* (New York, 1884), 87–88.
22. Weintraub, *Disraeli*, 301–2.
23. *Battling for Peace: A Memoir* (New York: Random House, 1995), 25.

3

Liberalism and Zionism (1986)

"Liberalism is always being surprised." That was how Lionel Trilling used to describe the characteristic liberal failure to imagine what reason and common sense appeared to gainsay. During the past century few things have surprised and offended the liberal imagination more than the weird persistence of the Jewish nation. Liberal friends of the Jews expected that their emancipation would put an end to Jewish collective existence. Count Stanislas de Clermont-Tonnerre, the French revolutionary, told the French National Assembly in 1789 that "the Jews should be denied everything as a nation, but granted everything as individuals." Wilhelm von Humboldt, the great liberal reformer of Prussia whose ethical idealism is celebrated in Mill's *On Liberty*, considered the disappearance of the Jews as a distinct group a condition for taking up the cause of their emancipation.

When the Jews failed to live up to their sponsors' expectations, the reaction against them could be fierce. George Eliot wrote in 1878 that modern English resentment of Jews for maintaining themselves in moral isolation from their fellow citizens was strongest among "liberal gentlemen" who "usually belong to a party which has felt itself glorified in winning for Jews ... the full privileges of citizenship." Eliot had herself once belonged to that party, and in 1848, when her revolutionary ardor was at its height, predicted that the Jews as a "race" were "plainly destined to extermination." But between 1848 and 1874, when she began to write *Daniel Deronda*, her liberalism was tempered by a wider experience of mankind and a deeper reflection on the meaning of nationality in general and of the organized memory of Jewish national consciousness in particular. She came to cherish the idea of "restoration of a Jewish State planted on the old ground," not only because it would afford the Jews a center of national feeling and a source of dignifying protection, but because it would contribute to the councils of the world "an added form of national genius," and one of transcendent (though not Christian) meaning. At the conclusion of her essay on the Jewish problem ("The Modern HEP! HEP! HEP!"), she pleads with Millite liberals to enlarge their master's ideal of individuality to include nations: "A modern book on Liberty has maintained that from the freedom of individual men to persist in idiosyncrasies the world may be enriched. Why should we not apply this argument to the idiosyncrasy of a nation, and pause in our haste to hoot it down?"

The relation among liberalism, democracy, and the Jewish nation is directly addressed in two ambitious books on Zionism and Israel by liberals. Bernard Avishai, author of *The Tragedy of Zionism* and self-styled elegist of Zionism, has cast himself in the role of Epimenides coming to Athens, or Plato to Syracuse, sternly ignoring the contemptible traditional and local idiosyncrasies of the natives in order to bestow on them the blessings of "British liberal tradition," "secular democracy," "liberal decency," and "a written constitution." Unlike Epimenides and Plato, who landed before dispensing advice, Avishai is doing so from afar, long after having departed Israel. In his prologue he describes how, in 1972, he and his wife left Canada to become Israelis. But by 1973 they began to feel that they were victims of "cultural enslavement" whose "English spirit" was being blotted out by Hebrew. The instrument of their unconversion from Zionism was television; American and English programs revealed to them that they were "living among foreigners" and that their true home, to which they soon returned, was Canada and the English language.

Although he momentarily blamed himself for failing to become an Israeli, Avishai quickly decided that the blame lay with Israel, which, if you are American, turns your children into strangers, and with Zionism, which, "like old halachic norms," represses "individual life . . . equivocation, sexuality," desiderata of the "culture of liberalism" that he now pursues in Massachusetts. Five pages after describing how he saved himself from the clearest and most dangerous siren call he had ever heard, Avishai announces that it is time "to retire" Zionism in favor of democracy. Ten pages later he contemptuously describes political Zionists such as Leo Pinsker, Theodor Herzl, and Vladimir Jabotinsky as people who invented an ideology to assuage "personal disappointment," for they "were themselves people who had tried to assimilate and . . . failed."[1] The ironic vision of this tragedian-elegist does not extend to himself.

16

Conor Cruise O'Brien also begins his massive study of Israel and Zionism, called *The Siege*, by describing those elements in his national, religious, and family background that drew him to the subject. In the late 1950s that most unphilosophical principle called the alphabet conspired with destiny to situate O'Brien, as Ireland's UN representative, between Iraq and Israel, a revealing perspective for a shrewd observer. In 1961 he left Ireland's foreign service but subsequently went into politics at home, where he served four years in the opposition and four years as a member of the Irish government. He is a liberal, but it was not his liberalism that made him see the return to Zion, which took place under "harsher necessities" than any ever imagined by liberals, as "the greatest story of modern times." As an Irish Catholic he had no trouble recognizing, at the heart of Zionism, a powerful bond between religion and nationality. As the child of a lapsed or "enlightened" Catholic father, whom he labels a *maskil* (Hebrew for "enlightened one"), O'Brien grew up sufficiently "alienated" from Catholic society to feel yet another link with Jews living as strangers in Exile. Finally, he was moved by the conviction that "Irish Catholics . . . have had a greater experience of persecution, oppression and stigmatization than any other people in Western Europe *except* the Jews."[2]

Throughout his book O'Brien freely and candidly uses his experience as an Irishman and a diplomat to shed coruscating light on the story of the Zionist movement as well as on the play of forces around that movement. This means that in his view of the Mandatory government, the British Anglo-Saxon constitutional system, which to Avishai is a second (and superior) revelation from Sinai, sometimes appears to be just what Matthew Arnold called it: "a colossal machine for the manufacture of Philistines." O'Brien remarks that among such Philistines "antisemitism is a light sleeper" and offers as an instance the use in British official circles, starting in 1941, of the epithet "Jewish Nazi state."[3] For Avishai, antisemitic remarks by Ernest Bevin (British foreign minister 1945–51) are "tactlessness," something akin to eating soup with a fork.[4]

O'Brien's saga of Israel and Zionism is in two volumes. The first recounts the story of Zionism from the assassination of Czar Alexander II through the expiration of the British Mandate in 1948 and includes detailed analysis of the whole spectrum of Zionist ideologies; portraits of such central actors as Herzl, Weizmann, Ben-Gurion, and Jabotinsky; and accounts of the Dreyfus Affair, Eastern European pogroms, and British motives and actions in Palestine. The second, longer volume

tells the story of Israel from its bloody beginning through the comple-
tion of the withdrawal from Lebanon in summer 1985. It comprises
lengthy chapters on the inner life of Israel as expressed in its literature, on Israel's Oriental Jewish population, on the Arabs of Israel and
the administered territories, and on the complex relations between
international diplomacy and Israel's wars. *The Siege* is the work of a
writer of open, flexible intelligence and boundless curiosity. The book
therefore has a kind of noble imperfection, like that of large Victorian
novels lovingly called loose and baggy monsters.

Avishai's "tragedy," by contrast, has the completeness of a limited
mind. The first part of the book analyzes the development of Zionist
ideas, especially in relation to certain crossroads in the development
of the *yishuv* (Palestinian Jewish community), with favorable emphasis
on cultural as opposed to political Zionism. The second part of this
book traces, in just three chapters, the rapid disintegration of Labor
Zionism from its victory at the 1931 World Zionist Congress to "the
end of Zionism" on the eve of the Six-Day War. The last, most aggressively polemical, section of the book presents the various tragedies
and failures, from 1967 to the present, that resulted from Ben-Gurion's
"post-Zionist matrix" of "power, Bible, defiance, settlement, economic
growth." Avishai's is a much narrower book than O'Brien's in scope
because it tells comparatively little of what the gentiles, apart from
Palestinian Arabs, are thinking and doing. His description of the 1938
Evian conference on Jewish refugees, for example, includes a polite,
passing allusion to the failure of the Western democracies to accept
Jews, followed by a detailed, acerbic description of Labor Zionist hopes
that the conference would fail. This is also a narrower book in its quality
of mind. O'Brien's discussion of Israeli literature ranges widely from
Abba Kovner, Aharon Appelfeld, David Shahar, and Yehuda Amichai to
Amos Oz and A. B. Yehoshua. Avishai's discussion is limited to books
and plays that illustrate "the liberal, post-Zionist curve of Israel's leading writers," especially if these writers deal with an Arab-Jewish love
affair or depict Israelis as Nazis.[5]

Both books are unusually personal and enlivened by anecdote.
O'Brien's invocations of experience often reveal the hypocrisy or hatred
that is part of the burden Israel must bear. Recalling how in 1974 the UN
delegates of every Western European nation, including Ireland, joined
in the standing ovation for Arafat, O'Brien says, "I asked our Foreign
Minister, Garret FitzGerald, whether it was altogether wise for Ireland
to be so fulsome about the P.L.O.: might there not be a precedent in

relation to the I.R.A.? Garret thought not . . . Arafat and his Fatah were the moderates." On another occasion, as Ireland's representative at the 1946 conference on refugees in Geneva, O'Brien had to meet with a monsignor representing the Vatican who frankly told his interlocutor of his feelings about Jews: "I'm not antisemitic. I just hate them."[6] Avishai's anecdotes serve mainly to cast a warm glow over his debating skills marshaled in combat against illiberal, paranoiac Jews. In Israel he vanquished a taxi driver whose experiences in Lebanon had embittered him toward Palestinian Arabs. In North America he joined an Israeli in heaping scorn on Diaspora Jews who still brood over the Holocaust and "now need to invent anti-Semites to feel like Jews, to perform the commandment of Auschwitz." (It is characteristic of Avishai to suppose that the power exercised over ordinary Jews by Emil Fackenheim's commandment not to give Hitler posthumous victories is merely that of a smart syllogism, on the order of "since Hitler didn't want Jews in Germany, we must live there."[7])

The stark contrast in method, tenor, and tone between the two books is everywhere apparent. For O'Brien the Jews, for all their political ineptitude, are a great people, and the state of Israel, despite its "Panglossian" professors; proud, overweening politicians; and a national character "so democratic as to be almost unworkable," is the culmination of a movement whose power over gentiles as well as Jews is a "mystery" that cannot be explained except by the divine power of the Bible. For Avishai, full of acrid contempt for those who sense "something mysterious and wonderful about Jewish history," the Jews are a small people, but a nasty one. Their country has become the devil's own experiment station, where the state is "superior to all other moral values," where young people increasingly succumb to their primordial instincts for "domination, lockstep, revenge," and where the Bible impedes peace by deluding "new" Zionists into calling the West Bank "Judea and Samaria" (always enclosed by the author in whining quotation marks) and impedes "liberal democracy" by imposing on Hebrew speakers an archaic vocabulary in which the word for "freedom" (cherut) is national rather than individual in meaning. O'Brien expresses admiration for the heroism of the outnumbered Jewish defenders of the settlements of Yad Mordechai, Degania (helpfully identified by Avishai as Umm Juni, its Arab name), and Geulim. Citing several sources, he writes that in the War of Independence "the numbers actually engaged on the two sides seem to have been about equal. But the Arabs had a huge initial superiority in . . . equipment and firepower, heavy weapons, armor and aircraft." Avishai, judging the efforts of the Jews by the severe conceptions of gallantry prevalent at MIT, where he teaches, is unimpressed. He writes, citing no sources at all, that "Jewish forces outnumbered the combined strength of the Arab forces and Palestinian irregulars by 2 to 1—a fact which should dispel misty notions about how courage alone vanquished the Arab Goliath."[8]

In both books the immigration to Israel in the 1950s of large numbers of Oriental Jews, strangers to democracy, receives detailed attention. O'Brien describes the lives these people led as second-class citizens in their lands of origin, where they were held in contempt by the aggressive "trimphalist creed" of Islam. He argues persuasively that they were something more than a mixed multitude, incapable of appreciating the socialism and atheism of Israel's founders. Rather, they were Zionists, from "national traditions kept alive through religious observance." For Avishai, the Oriental Jews were not merely, like many of the children of Labor Zionist veterans, not Zionists; they were also destitute of liberalism, hence poor material for secular democracy. It was in order to mobilize such a rabble, he argues, that Ben-Gurion had to sacrifice the revolutionary ideas of Labor Zionism in favor of statism and militarism, and diplomacy in favor of retaliation. The best of the Oriental Jews, that is, their "liberal intelligentsia," had gone to Montreal or New York rather than Israel, and the rest were deaf to the blandishments of socialism and democracy. Incapable of appreciating "secular categories," they came to Israel because it afforded them a "chance to be strong against the Arabs." Explicitly, Avishai bewails the fact that so few Yemenite cobblers and North African policemen have learned the true, "European" meanings of democracy and freedom at Hebrew University; implicitly, what bothers him is that so many have learned about Arabs from experience and not from, say, the country's institutes of Middle East studies, where they would have received instruction in how to hallucinate moderation in their enemies,[9] an exercise that usually brings the same result as hallucinating an oasis in the middle of a desert.

Ascribing moderation to the enemies of Israel and blind, willful extremism to its leaders is characteristic of Avishai's approach. There are assorted "tragedies" scattered through his account of Zionism, starting with the Histadrut (General Federation of Jewish Workers) establishment of a "dictatorship of the proletariat." But for Avishai the underlying meaning of "tragedy" is that the protagonist, Zionism, has brought about its own destruction by *hamartia* ("arrogant pride"). He describes King Feisal of Iraq in 1919 "offer[ing] protection for Zionism under a united Arab state." O'Brien points out that the real intent of the agreement with Chaim Weizmann was, as even the Royal Commission Report of 1937 confirmed, that "if King Hussein and Emir Feisal secured their big Arab state, they would concede little Palestine to the Jews." The agreement, wrote a British intelligence officer, Colonel French, at the time of its signing, "is not worth the paper it is written on." Avishai depicts the present King Hussein of Jordan intrepidly arguing for recognition of Israel at the Khartoum conference of Arab nations following the Six-Day War. But how, asks Avishai, could he dream of making peace without getting back Jerusalem? We are not told why Hussein showed no interest in peace or recognition between 1953, when he came to the throne, and 1967, when he led his country into war against Israel. In any event, the ascendant political figure in Israel by this time was Moshe Dayan, who, allegedly, made any settlement impossible. For Avishai, Dayan is "a modern pharaoh" who virtually created Palestinian Arab "radicalism." So fond is Avishai of this conceit whereby (in the familiar style of Arab propaganda) Arabs become Jews and Israelis their gentile oppressors that he tells how Dayan's heart, like Pharaoh's, "had been hardened by terrorist attacks such as the one at Ma'alot." This is to say that Arafat does not murder but only executes divine sentence. Avishai claims that "in 1968, Arafat was still an unlikely guerrilla, crisscrossing the West Bank on a motorcycle." O'Brien, however, reminds us that in March 1968, at Karameh, this pathetically enterprising cyclist, in league with a Hussein who now called himself a *fedayee*, murdered twenty-three Israeli soldiers. Avishai indignantly reports that in 1976 only the dove Yossi Sarid recognized that the newly elected pro-PLO mayors of the West Bank, graciously willing to set up a state "in whatever part of the homeland would be liberated," represented "a new opportunity for Israeli diplomacy." O'Brien quotes "moderate" Palestinian Arabs who unblushingly declare that "the step that follows liberation is the dismantling of the racist . . . structure of Israel as a state." He offers, too, the sobering reminder that the organizers of the massacre of Israeli schoolchildren at Ma'alot "were well-known Palestinian 'moderates' who had been in dialogue with Israeli 'doves.'"[10]

Avishai's generosity toward Israel's adversaries is epistemological as well as political. He sneers at claims of Revisionist Zionists that most Palestinian Arabs were as much immigrants to the country as most Jews were. He does not deny the fact, but argues that Arabs who moved to Palestine from Damascus or Amman were, "in their own eyes, . . . doing no more than moving from one part of the Arab homeland to another." How such people could consistently also claim, after 1948, to be homeless refugees if they lived anywhere outside the borders of Israel is not a question to interest Avishai, though he castigates Labor Zionists for causing the displacement of Arab residents "from their country." Later he refers gingerly to Joan Peters's "highly controversial book" about Arab immigration to Palestine, promising that a friend of his—the infamous Norman Finkelstein—will soon explode Peters's thesis. But in the meantime we must rest content with the view that "the number of Arabs who came, and their actual place of origin, beg the question of the subjective feelings of the people who came to call themselves Palestinians." That is to say, it does not much matter what things are in themselves, but only what they appear to be to Arabs.[11]

O'Brien points out that among the "subjective feelings" of Israel's Arab adversaries, belief in Enlightenment principles of secular democracy barely exists. Nevertheless, it is in this language that they have chosen to make their case to the West, knowing that it will be music to the inward ear of liberals. "In terms of the governing code of debate, based on the Western Enlightenment value system, this puts the Arab states—and the cause of Government by Consent—permanently in the right, and Israel—with its archaic Right of Return and Jewish State—permanently in the wrong." Of course, O'Brien adds, Muslim spokesmen who appeal to Enlightenment principles "are engaging in double-talk, masking the realities of what is fundamentally, on both sides, a religious-nationalist culture conflict." He notes that the terrorist group *Fatah*, whose spokesmen repeat "secular democratic state" with the regularity of a steam engine, is an organization whose name means the opening of a country for conquest by Islam.[12] The archetype of the relation of Palestinian Arabs to democracy is for O'Brien their outright rejection of the Palestine Constitution proposed by Palestine High Commissioner Herbert Samuel and Colonial Secretary Winston Churchill in 1922. Although Weizmann accepted this commitment to representative democracy, the Arab majority scorned an arrangement that did not abolish the Balfour Declaration and bestow on them the power to exclude Jews from Palestine. Then, as now, only "the prestige of the absolute" could enrapture Palestinian Arabs.[13]

For both writers the nature of democracy in Israel is bound up with religion; beyond that point they diverge in every particular. In the first part of his book, Avishai insists, often to the point of absurdity, on denying Jewish religion any role in the development of Zionism; but his account of events after 1948 alleges that religious influence poisoned Zionism, prevented territorial concession, and maimed by compression, like a Chinese lady's foot, every libertarian impulse of Israeli citizens. On the very first page of his tragedy, Avishai states that Czar Nicholas I "had been dismayed by Jewish sympathies for Napoleon's occupation."[14] The statement is typical Avishai for two reasons. First, it is wrong. Nicholas, not famous for his love of Jews, wrote of them in his diary: "Surprisingly . . . in 1812 they were very loyal to us and assisted us in every possible way even at the risk of their own lives."[15] Second, it is wrong because Avishai cannot admit that, given the choice, many Jews preferred their traditional religious observance under a tyrant to emancipation under the aegis of French Enlightenment.

Avishai's account of the origins of Zionism is diametrically opposed to that of O'Brien, who insists that Jewish nationalism drew its ultimate strength from Jewish religion and that even Ben-Gurion and Weizmann were, and could not but be, essentially religious Jews. Avishai never even mentions such early religious Zionists as Yehudah Alkalai and the widely read Zevi Hirsch Kalischer; he declares that the Eretz Yisrael of religious Jews "corresponded to no actual territory," even though Weizmann had somehow got the impression that Jews in the East End of London who prayed for dew in the summer and rain in the winter were attached to Palestine (and not Atlantis); and he reports (falsely) that all religious Zionists at the congresses supported Herzl's scheme for emergency settlement of Jews in Uganda. He lashes Ben-Gurion and Golda Meir for not entering into a *Kulturkampf* against religious forces. He depicts Rabbi Abraham Isaac Kook, who held out a welcoming hand to Labor Zionism, as a parasite, but reserves his harshest epithets for the new, religious Zionists who do work the land. Although Avishai's single reference to Jewish daily prayers—"the daily prayers stated that Jews had been exiled 'for their sins'"—indicates he has not said them for a long time, he is filled with a visceral loathing for those who do, which reminds one that the French Enlightenment, whose child he is, was not only liberal and secular—it was also antisemitic. "Scripture hawks," "ultra-nationalist settlers," and "fringe romantics"—these people have, in Avishai's view, lost the human status.[16]

The relatively small number of religious Jews in the fledgling state and the much larger number of citizens for whom religious symbols had become, through the agency of the state, a kind of civil religion kept Israel from becoming a secular, democratic state in two ways, according

to Avishai. First, they made it impossible to promulgate a comprehen-
sive bill of rights and constitution, and thus enabled the discriminatory
Law of Return, which grants citizenship to all Jews who request it, to be
passed and maintained. In the long list of liberal nostrums prescribed by
Avishai for the de-Judaization of Israel, abolition of the Law of Return
has a high place. He is not, however, a dogmatic egalitarian; he does
not want Arabs to be bothered with that little matter of serving in the
army from the age of eighteen to fifty-five, and he does not object to
the principle of "affirmative action" as such. In fact, he recommends
it—for the Arabs. Second, the religious and their allies stand accused
of fostering an atmosphere of intolerance, especially in Israeli schools,
that permeates all aspects of society. For his information on the "anti-
democratic views" of Israeli high school students, Avishai relies on the
tendentious polls conducted by Jerusalem's leftist Van Leer Institute,
Israel's version of the Institute for Policy Studies. His complaint that
"Israeli schools have taught children much more about the tribes of
Israel than about the Enlightenment" will elicit a bitter laugh from
people whose children have actually attended these schools, the kind
of laugh invited by one who cries fire in the midst of a flood.[17]

In his epilogue to *The Siege*, O'Brien argues cogently against exchang-
ing the territories of Judea and Samaria for an illusory peace. This notion can be espoused only by well-intentioned fools or ill-intentioned
rogues. By a strange irony, O'Brien adds, "Those in the West who urge
that the effort to rule over large numbers of Arabs may eventually
destroy Israel itself might do well to note that Meir Kahane is making
the same point, while drawing from it an inference radically different
from what the Western critics have in mind."[18] Avishai, who favors yet
another partitioning of Palestine, "the only democratic solution," is not
exactly making "the same point" as Kahane, yet there is an uncanny
resemblance between the mental worlds they inhabit. In both, the
opposition between Zionism and democracy is inevitable and Man-
ichaean. In both, the "problem" of marriage between Jew and Arab is
obsessive. Kahane wants to outlaw it, and Avishai, speaking for those
few Israelis who combine the liberal craving for forbidden fruit with
the liberal craving for legality, wants Israel to institute civil marriage.[19]

In flagellating Israel with half-understood, misapplied, and uniquely
inappropriate slogans about the "tyranny of the majority" that he has
gleaned from Tocqueville and Mill, while demanding that Israel surrender its Jewish character, Avishai shows a poor grasp not just of his liberal
sources (for whom "liberal" democracy was nearly an oxymoron),[20]

but of something far more important. Mill once wrote that in the makeup of every state there must be "*something* which is settled, something permanent, and not to be called in question: something which, by general agreement, has a right to be where it is, and to be secure against disturbance."[21] In the state of the Jews, a state (as O'Brien keeps stressing) under siege and likely to remain so, that "something" can never be liberalism but only Jewish religion, a Judaism freely and variously interpreted, but always including the conviction that Jewish life leads somewhere because it began somewhere. Men live and, if need be, die for values, not for procedures; for beliefs, not for conclusions. This religion may not suit the most refined tastes, and some of its devotees may be raw and blind in their gropings. Early Labor Zionists seemed to do very well without it because, as O'Brien recognizes, they were sustained by the very religion they denied. The same was not true for their children and grandchildren, for whom no traditional faith existed that could endow gestures of rebellion with meaning.

It is a gloomy thought that the enemies of Israel neither slumber nor sleep. But there is comfort, too, in remembering that the first elegist to crow over the demise of Zion was a fellow named Merneptah, a ruler of Egypt who announced that "Israel is desolated; its seed is no more." That was in the year 1215 BCE.

Notes

1. Bernard Avishai, *The Tragedy of Zionism* (New York: Farrar, Straus, Giroux, 1985), 6, 12, 25, 230, 309, 319.
2. Conor Cruise O'Brien, *The Siege: The Saga of Israel and Zionism*, 2 vols. (London: Weidenfeld and Nicolson, 1986), 21, 18–19, 329–30, 656. In her essay "The Modern HEP! HEP! HEP!" George Eliot likened the situation of the Jews among the English to that of the Irish. The Jews are blamed for rejecting Christianity, the Irish for rejecting Protestantism. "'No Irish need apply,' parallels the sentence which for many polite persons sums up the question of Judaism, 'I never *did* like the Jews.'"
3. O'Brien, *Siege*, 258.
4. Avishai, *Tragedy of Zionism*, 170. Avishai is equally charitable toward the constitutional democracies of the U.S. and Canada, which, he says, closed their doors to mass immigration "in the depths of economic depression." In fact, those doors were closed in the boom years of the twenties. Irving Abella and Harold Troper (*None Is Too Many*) have demonstrated that Canada's distinction of admitting fewer Jewish refugees from Hitler than any other Western country had nothing to do with economics, and everything to do with that "tactlessness" called antisemitism.
5. Avishai, *Tragedy of Zionism*, 152, 301, 313, 321–22.
6. O'Brien, *Siege*, 485, 266.

7. Avishai, *Tragedy of Zionism*, 309, 352–53.

8. Ibid., 221, 249–50, 180, 309; O'Brien, *Siege*, 18, 153, 291, 443, 540. According to American military historian Trevor Dupuy, the Arabs committed 40,000 men to the conflict; the Jews had 30,000 under arms, and 10,000 more ready for mobilization.

9. O'Brien, *Siege*, 348; Avishai, 210–11.

10. O'Brien, *Siege*, 144, 479, 462; Avishai, *Tragedy of Zionism*, 106, 275, 277, 280.

11. Avishai, *Tragedy of Zionism*, 140, 148, 368n8. The best account of the controversy over Joan Peters's *From Time Immemorial: The Origins of the Arab-Jewish Conflict over Palestine* (New York: Harper & Row, 1984) is the essay "Whose Palestine?" by Erich Isaac and Rael Jean Isaac in *Commentary* 81 (July 1986): 29–37. See also "'Whose Palestine?'—An Exchange," in *Commentary* 82 (October 1986): 2–22.

12. O'Brien, *Siege*, 654–55. Avishai's Palestinian Arabs not only appear indifferent to religion; the ones living in Israel are reported to be powerfully attracted to "Israel's libertarian style of life" (Avishai, *Tragedy of Zionism*, 317). Apparently, if we believe anything Avishai says about Israel's illiberalism, Israeli Arabs are easily satisfied.

13. O'Brien, *Siege*, 162–64.

14. Avishai, 15.

15. Simon Dubnow, *History of the Jews in Russia and Poland*, 3 vols. (1916; repr., New York: KTAV, 1975), 2:14.

16. Avishai, *Tragedy of Zionism*, 20, 65, 94, 252, 285–86, 323.

17. Ibid., 189, 319–20, 305. The biased and unreliable character of Van Leer surveys has been analyzed by Professor Shlomo Sharan of Tel Aviv University (see *Ma' ariv*, International Edition, September 27, 1985).

18. O'Brien, *Siege*, 649–50.

19. Avishai, *Tragedy of Zionism*, 9.

20. In a letter from 1855, Mill wrote, "Almost all the projects of social reformers of these days are really liberticide."

21. J. S. Mill, "Coleridge," in *Autobiography and Other Writings*, ed. Jack Stillinger, Riverside ed. (Boston: Houghton Mifflin, 1969), 276.

4

What the Holocaust Does *Not* Teach (1993)

"World Jewry has a special responsibility." This hectoring trumpet call blared forth from the midst of a *New York Times* op-ed piece (November 9, 1992) by Flora Lewis entitled "Save Lives in Bosnia." Jews, she argued, had acquired this special responsibility to Bosnian survivors of Serbian camps because their own ancestors had experienced concentration camps; now they had the opportunity "to show that concentration camps provoke the solidarity of victims of persecution." For Lewis, the lesson of the Holocaust is that Jews now have a responsibility to behave particularly well because their ancestors suffered so much persecution. The unstated corollary of this argument (as Conor Cruise O'Brien once pointed out in another context) is that the descendants of people who have not been persecuted do not have a special responsibility to behave particularly well, and the descendants of the persecutors of Jews can be excused altogether for behavior that would be very hard to excuse in other people. That is perhaps why Lewis went on to give specific instructions to Jews to offer Bosnian Muslims refuge in Israel in order to show "that the Jewish state does indeed want to get on in peace with its Muslim neighbors." Since the ancestors of these Muslim neighbors did their very best to choke off Jewish immigration to Palestine during World War II, it follows, according to Lewis's immaculate logic, that these Arab neighbors should now not only be excused for their recent attempts to keep Soviet and Ethiopian Jews from reaching Israel, but should also be offered this conciliatory gesture (which can be expected to have a mighty impact on nations that have always treated *Arab* refugees like human refuse).

If this seems rather a peculiar lesson to extract from the Holocaust, it is sobriety itself when compared with some that have been expounded by even more nimble interpreters. In Israel, one of the few places in the world where the "special responsibility" of Jews is discussed more frequently than in the editorial pages of the *New York Times*, the new minister of education, Shulamit Aloni, has taken it upon herself to reverse the direction of that country's study and commemoration of the Holocaust. A generation ago Israel's greatest writers, from Uri Zvi Greenberg on the right to Abba Kovner on the left, exhorted their countrymen to look backward and reflect upon the impetus they had received from the experience of the Nazi murder of European Jewry and the callous indifference of the nations of the world to the Jewish catastrophe, and to consider their responsibility to redeem the dead. "From the promised land I called you," wrote Kovner in poetic address to the murdered children of Europe: "I looked for you/among heaps of small shoes. / At every approaching holiday." Gershom Scholem, in *The Messianic Idea in Judaism*, justified the choice of the Star of David for the Israeli flag precisely because "under this sign [the Jews] were murdered," and "the sign which . . . has been sanctified by suffering and dread has become worthy of illuminating the path to life and reconstruction."[1] In 1970 he predicted, in an essay in *Ariel*, that "the reaction to the Holocaust, when it comes, could be either deadly or productive. We hope it will be productive; that is why we are living here, in this Land."[2]

But Mrs. Aloni, the Israeli version of what East European Jews used to call "a cossack in a sukkah," has deplored the stress upon the Holocaust as regressive and nationalistic. "I do not take pictures of the backside of history," she declared on Israeli Radio. "The Ministry of Education must be concerned with the future." Even before her elevation to office, Aloni had frequently denounced Holocaust education in Israel because it taught children that "the Nazis did this to the Jews instead of the message that people did this to people." If Mrs. Aloni has her way in the Israeli schools, then the Nazi murder of the Jews of Europe, a crime of terrifying clarity and distinctness, a crime based on the principle that every European must be able to prove that he is *not* a Jew in order to claim the right to live, will become for young Israelis a blurred, amorphous agony, an indeterminate part of man's inhumanity to man.

Do the ratiocinations of Lewis and Aloni confirm the wisdom of replying to the question of what we learn from the Holocaust with the dismissive quip: "Nothing, I hope"? The late Lucy Dawidowicz would not have thought so. In her posthumously published collection of essays, *What Is the Use of Jewish History?*, she returns frequently to this question, most notably in "How They Teach the Holocaust" and "Could America Have Rescued Europe's Jews?" The former, a survey of how the Holocaust is taught in American secondary schools, shows that some American Holocaust curricula have already achieved the condition to which Aloni would have the (putatively Jewish) Israeli schools aspire. One used excerpts from *Mein Kampf* not just to show that "racist hatred extends to all groups that are 'others'" but to give the impression that blacks and not Jews were Hitler's primary targets. The most pervasive failure of these curricula, Dawidowicz discovered, was omission of the long history of antisemitism, with the term itself generally subsumed under the generic "racism and prejudice."[3] Dawidowicz never doubted that we study the history of the murder of the European Jews not only to mourn and remember them, but to try to understand and learn lessons from the past. The past could not, however, instruct those who asked it the wrong questions. The unrelenting ferocity of her attack on historian David Wyman, who in *The Abandonment of the Jews* asked the question "Could America Have Rescued Europe's Jewry?", arose not so much from a desire to defend Roosevelt and American Jewry from allegations of complicity in the Holocaust as from a flinty political realism. Not for her the imagined otherwise of what she derisively labeled "preaching History" (176), which made moral judgments on the basis of the *ought* rather than the *is* of history.

The real question to ask, she insisted, was how the country called Nazi Germany could have quickly gained dominion over Europe and readily enlisted both its own citizens and other peoples into mass murder of the people called the Jews. Judicious answers to *this* question, she asserted, would suggest the lessons to be learned from the Holocaust. The first was the infectious power of antisemitism, especially when embodied in the state; the second was the importance of a strong military (for if the pacifists, appeasers, and isolationists had not first had *their* way in England and America, Hitler would not have had *his* way in Europe); the third, "one which every Jewish child now knows" (177), was the necessity of Jewish political power and a Jewish state for Jewish survival.

Those who reject these lessons have a vested interest in opposing study of the Holocaust or distorting its history. Given Shulamit Aloni's insistence that it was not the Nazis who murdered the Jews but "people [who] did this to people," it would not have surprised Dawidowicz (or, for that matter, Gershom Scholem) to learn that Aloni has also blamed

Jews for arousing antisemitism in Poland by displaying the flag of the Jewish state at Auschwitz and for other Holocaust-related activities "which create the feeling that we were victims and that we have to be strong." Apparently, the wisdom Dawidowicz attributed to every Jewish child has not yet reached every Jewish adult.

Notes

1. *The Messianic Idea in Judaism* (New York: Schocken, 1971), 281.
2. "Reflections on the Possibility of Jewish Mysticism in Our Time," *Ariel* 26 (Spring 1970): 46.
3. *What Is the Use of Jewish History*, ed. Neal Kozodoy (New York: Schocken, 1992), 70–73. Subsequent reference to this work will appear parenthetically in the text.

5

Why Jews Must Behave Better than Everybody Else: The Theory and Practice of the Double Standard (1991)

In October 1989 the annual motion to expel Israel from the United Nations was brought to the floor of the General Assembly by the delegate from Libya. To him fell the privilege of denouncing Israel as an outlaw country unsuited to be a member in good standing of the family of nations. The incident calls to mind a dramatic moment in Philip Roth's novel *The Counterlife* when a metalworker named Buki says, "I am in Norway on business for my product and written on a wall I read: 'Down with Israel!' I think, what did Israel ever do to Norway? I know Israel is a terrible country but, after all, there are countries even more terrible. . . . Why don't you read on Norwegian walls, 'Down with Russia,' 'Down with Chile,' 'Down with Libya'? Because Hitler didn't murder six million Libyans? I am walking in Norway and I am thinking, 'If only he had.' Because then they would write on Norwegian walls, 'Down with Libya,' and leave Israel alone."

But this opening of the UN General Assembly was driven from the front page by something even more calamitous: namely, the Bay Area earthquake. The earthquake interrupted the World Series, and in the aftermath of so much destruction and suffering the question arose, should the games continue? The commissioner of baseball, recognizing the sensitivity of the situation, postponed the third game for eleven days. Several sportswriters noted that this action was in sharp contrast to that of Avery Brundage, chairman of the International Olympic

31

Committee, who, about two hours after eleven Israeli athletes had been murdered by PLO terrorists during the Munich Olympics of 1972, declared that "the games must go on." Brundage's reasoning may have been something like that imputed to Roth's Norwegian graffiti artist, for in 1936 the same Brundage, as chairman of the American Olympic Committee, had insisted that—despite the little unpleasantnesses to which Jews in Germany were then being subjected—he could find no hard evidence that Germany was discriminating against its Jewish athletes, and therefore "the games must go on."

One notable feature of the postmortems on the Israeli athletes in 1972 was the fear expressed by the man in charge of the ABC television crew broadcasting the games. His greatest concern of the moment, he said, was not for the athletes who had just been murdered—not for him such banal emotions—but for what might result from what he called the wellknown Israeli propensity to exact an eye for an eye and a tooth for a tooth. He thus became one of the first moralists to establish the by now well-fixed principle that the conjectural potentiality of what Israelis *might* do is a more legitimate occasion for grief than the actuality of what Arabs have *already* done. Thus the *Washington Post*, in the spring of 1984, printed a photo of a dead Israeli woman, slumped in the seat of the bus she had been riding when an Arab terrorist's bomb ended her life, and commented, "A woman was one of three persons killed yesterday when a bomb exploded on an Israeli bus in the latest incident of a growing wave of violence that was expected to raise fears about retaliation against Arabs." In ordinary cases of murder, sympathy is generally directed to the murdered person; when Israelis are murdered, sympathy is directed, with remarkable frequency, either to the conjectural victim of Jewish retaliation or to the murderer himself, who was driven to commit his deeds because he had not been listened to sufficiently.

In February 1978 an ABC TV program called *Hostage* examined the terrorist use of hostages to achieve political ends. The stars of the program were Palestinian Arabs and their supporters. From start to finish the narrator took it for granted that in any terrorist outrage it is not the victim—the mutilated child or murdered mother—but the terrorist himself who is the injured party, and whose grievances require immediate healing. In November of the same year, Frank Reynolds of ABC justified an hour-long commercial for violence entitled "Terror in the Promised Land" by claiming that the Palestinian Arabs had been forced to kill people because no one would "listen" to them: "To refuse to listen is to strengthen their argument that violence is their only recourse."

Needless to say, those viewers whose memories had not atrophied in the preceding eight months understood just the opposite to be the case: the more they are "listened" to, the more clearly do terrorists recognize the profitability of murder. For in between their two prime-time shows on ABC, the Arab terrorists found time to commit some of their most spectacular outrages, including the murder in March of thirty-five men, women, and children, and the wounding of seventy others, on the coastal road near Haifa. Eight years later, in May 1986, by which time the Palestinian Arabs had surely become the most publicized claimants to victim status of any national or ethnic group in the world, Palestinian Arab terrorists butchered Pan Am passengers in Karachi and Jews worshiping in Istanbul. At this moment, Bill Moyers, another advocate of the "listening" theory of terrorism, called for a massive effort to discover, with respect to the killers, "Who are these young men? What's happening out there to rouse their fury?" Since the primary wish of these young louts is to destroy Israel and the Jews who inhabit it and perhaps also the Jews who do not, how exactly did Moyers propose to abate their "fury"?

It requires no abstruse research to conclude that there is something irregular, startling, flagrant, and scandalous in the way that many prolific, world-class explainers deal with Israel. It is the way of false moral symmetry and the double standard. On the one hand, the actuality of crimes that have been committed by Arabs is yoked together, by a perverse metaphorical violence, with the potentiality of crimes that might be committed by Israelis; and, on the other hand, Israel's actual conduct is judged by a standard applied to no other nations, least of all the Arab states.

No more industrious laborer in this Goshen of duplicity can be found than the *New Yorker*'s (Jewish) Middle East expert, Milton Viorst. Viorst hailed the three noes of Khartoum (August 1967: no peace, no recognition, no negotiation) as a major breakthrough for peace because the Arab naysayers did not specifically call for the destruction of Israel. (Actually, they did, for they declared the need to recover "all occupied Arab territory.") Viorst has called the incessant terrorist war against Israel, sponsored by states whose combined military might approaches that of NATO, the last resort of the weak against the powerful. He has called the Yom Kippur War launched by the Arabs a limited-objective exercise, not threatening to "Israel itself or to its people." He has alleged, falsely of course, that Rabbi Kook (the first chief rabbi of modern Eretz Yisrael) advocated an *Arabenrein* Israel and a "Jewish jihad." Profoundly troubled by the conjectural potentiality of such anti-Arab actions, he has yet to deplore the actuality of *Judenrein* Saudi Arabia or Jordan, or the grim situation of Jews in Syria, a country he usually depicts as a model of trustworthiness and responsibility. Syria may once or twice have used some aggressive language toward Israel, but, he adds, there are "hawks on both sides." Since Israel deploys forces just outside its northern border in Lebanon, why, he asks, should anyone complain about Syrian occupation of two-thirds of that country, especially since Syria has a conjectural fear that it may one day find "an Israeli army sitting on its western frontier."[1]

Viorst interprets Israeli attachment to Judea and Samaria as a cynical preference for territories over peace; but he defends Egypt's insistence on every inch of the Sinai as not only understandable but admirable. In a November 1989 op-ed piece in the *New York Times*, Viorst concluded that Israel is to blame for the carnage and chaos in Lebanon, which to the untutored eye seems to involve Syrians and various factions of Lebanese Arabs. . . .

We come then to the question of the theoretical justification offered for the double standard by its practitioners. Many of them have grown tired of denying its existence, and have instead taken to arguing that it really is right that things should be wrong, because the more unfairly Israel is treated, the better off it will be. Anthony Lewis is probably the best-known exponent of this view. About ten years ago an irreverent reader of the *New York Times* nominated Lewis for the Pete Rose Journalism Award, in recognition of his having written forty-four consecutive columns on the Arab-Israeli conflict that laid all blame for its continuance on the intransigence, brutality, and oppressiveness of the Jews. By now, even the Joe DiMaggio Award (for hits in fifty-six consecutive contests against Israel) would be insufficient recognition of Lewis's unmatched consistency in depicting Israel as a breeding ground of fanatics who have betrayed the high ideals of Jews of the prophetic persuasion, from Isaiah to Brandeis to Anthony Lewis himself.

Lewis typically deplores Israeli actions not merely because they hurt Arabs. No—he deplores them because they "cannot serve the spirit of Israel, or its true security." Like Brutus brooding over the misdeeds of his beloved Caesar, Lewis has persuaded himself that "in the spirit of men there is no blood." He is therefore not tremendously perturbed by the prospect that it may be difficult to come by

Israel's spirit without dismembering Israel. "Yes," Lewis has written, "there is a double standard. From its birth Israel asked to be judged as a light among nations."[2] Of course this preposterous assertion bears no relation to the truth about the Zionist movement, which rejected Jewish chosenness and sought precisely to normalize Jewish existence while gaining acceptance as a member of the family of nations, treated neither worse nor better than others. "Yes," said Jabotinsky to the Royal Commission in 1937, "we do want a state; every nation on earth, every normal nation, beginning with the smallest and humblest who do not claim any merit, any role in humanity's development—they all have states of their own. That is the normal condition for a people. Yet, when we ask for the same condition as the Albanians enjoy, then it is called too much. I would remind you of the commotion that was produced in that famous institution when Oliver Twist came and asked for 'more.' He said 'more' because he did not know how to express it; what Oliver really meant was this: 'Will you just give me that normal portion which is necessary for a boy of my age to be able to live?'"[3] Lewis's formulation is, finally, sinister in its insinuation that Israel has no right to exist unless and until it is perfect, a "light unto the nations," and therefore that it should never have been created in the first place.

In Anthony Trollope's novel of 1855, *The Warden*, a journalist named Tom Towers is described as "walking on from day to day, studiously trying to look like a man, but knowing within his heart that he was a god." In the Bible God himself keeps saying to Israel, "You only have I known among all the families of the earth; therefore, I will visit upon you all your iniquities" (Amos 3:2). In Lamentations Jeremiah describes how the enemy has ravaged Jerusalem and butchered its citizens, but conveys God's message that all is the fault of the Jews themselves. If God speaks as if he were a member of Peace Now, always blaming Israel for the aggression of its enemies, why should not the members and advocates of Peace Now speak as if *they* were God? In claiming that his invocation of the double standard to lacerate Israel for its sins arises from his unique love for her, Lewis has actually confused himself with the God of the Hebrew Bible, who also sees Israel as the only responsible party in Middle Eastern conflicts. Worship of one's own mind has rarely led to more flagrant idolatry.

Unless such idolatry be in the mind of Lewis's younger colleague at the *New York Times*, Thomas Friedman. In his widely acclaimed book *From Beirut to Jerusalem*, Friedman recounts a moment of revelation he had in London while reading the *International Herald Tribune*. He noticed that the paper had spread over four columns on its front page a photo of "an Israeli soldier not beating, not killing, but grabbing a Palestinian." When he sought out the story behind the photograph, he discovered only a two-paragraph item on page two. But the rude blare on the front page blotted out, among other small troubles in the Islamic world, that day's slaughter of several thousand people in the Iran-Iraq war. What, Friedman asked himself, was the explanation of this "lack of proportion"?

His answer was: "this unique double dimension" is attributable to "the historical and religious movements to which Israel is connected in Western eyes." The double standard of journalists covering the Middle East derives, according to Friedman, from their profound immersion in the Bible. Here, at last, is the explanation of the inveterate, obsessive lashing of Israel we have come to expect from G. A. Geyer, Robert Novak, and Nick Thimmesch on the right, or Tom Wicker, Christopher Hitchens, and Alexander Cockburn on the left: "Their identification with the dreams of Biblical Israel and mythic Jerusalem runs so deep, that when Israel succeeds and lives up to its prophetic expectations, it is their success too." It is because these journalists—most of whom must have been surprised to learn from Friedman of their profound identification with biblical Israel—view the world from a biblical perspective that they see the Jews as the central, decisive actors in the cosmic drama. Consequently, "what the West expects from the Jews of the past, it expects from Israel today."[4]

Is it possible that Thomas Friedman really believes that what the West expected of the Jews of the past was the perfection of so-called prophetic morality? Can this really be the same "West" whose Christian leaders, from the time that Christianity became the state religion of Rome in the fourth century, hounded and persecuted Jews because they had murdered or continued stubbornly to "deny" the Son of God, and whose secular leaders expelled them on racial grounds or stood by passively while the Nazis murdered them en masse? Most people, including, I suspect, the very journalistic colleagues whom Friedman depicts as daily engrossed in devotional exercises, will remember that "the West," far from thinking of the Jews benignly and ideally, has viewed them as deicides dancing obscenely at the foot of the cross, crafty and diabolic vampires draining the blood of Christian children for their Passover matzot, and, in the words of Martin Luther, "torturers and persecutors of Christians all over the world."

In only one respect is Friedman right about the unchanging great expectations of the West from the Jews. Despite the fierce persecutions to which they were subject, the Jews for two thousand years did not resort to preventive attack, armed resistance, or retaliation. One of the reasons for Zionism was the desire to flout these great expectations of endless passivity. If Friedman wants an explanation for the double standard of journalists, he should seek it in their disappointment in that department. But he prefers to believe, with Anthony Lewis, that the more unfairly Israel is attacked, the better this will be for the Jewish soul. The ostensibly flattering practice of applying the highest standards of responsibility and guilt to Israel alone has practical consequences that readily indicate its special attractiveness to apologists for Palestinian Arab irredentism.

Of course, the theorists of the double standard are lying through their teeth both in what they assert about Jewish expectations of the West and Western expectations of the Jews. Having begun with the words of a Philip Roth character, let me end the same way, especially since Roth's characters are usually wiser than their author on the subject of Israel: "The fellows who say to you, 'I expect more of the Jews,' don't believe them. *They expect less.* What they are really saying is, 'Okay, we know you're a bunch of ravenous bastards, and given half the chance you'd eat up half the world. . . . We know all these things about you, and so we're going to get you now. And how? Every time you make a move, we're going to say, "But we expect *more* of Jews, Jews are supposed to behave *better*."' *Jews* are supposed to behave better? After all that has happened? Being only a thick-headed grease monkey, I would have thought that it was the *non-Jews* whose behavior could stand a little improvement. Why are *we* the only people who belong to this wonderful exclusive moral club?"

Notes

1. David Bar-Illan, "Milton Viorst: Master of the Double Standard," in *With Friends Like These: The Jewish Critics of Israel*, ed. Edward Alexander (New York: SPI Books, 1993), 77–83.
2. See Ruth R. Wisse, "The Delegitimation of Israel," *Commentary*, 74 (July 1982), 29–36.
3. Evidence Submitted to the Palestine Royal Commission (1937), quoted in *The Zionist Idea*, ed. Arthur Hertzberg (New York: Atheneum, 1975), 559–70.
4. Thomas Friedman, *From Beirut to Jerusalem* (New York: Farrar, Straus & Giroux, 1989), See review by Martin Peretz in *New Republic*, 4 September 1989.

6

The Moral Failure of American Jewish Intellectuals: Past and Present (2013, 2014)

I: 1933–48

"Shame and contrition, because we have not done enough, weigh even more heavily upon the Jews of the free countries [than on the Allied powers]. Not only do we have the greater responsibility of kinsmen, but our own weakness may be one of the causes why so little has been done. The history of our times will one day make bitter reading, when it records that some Jews were so morally uncertain that they denied they were obligated to risk their own safety in order to save other Jews who were being done to death abroad."

—Ben Halpern, "We and the European Jews," *Jewish Frontier*, August 1943

Early in 1963 the controversy over a single book made it clear how much American Jews were still living "abroad," in both the shadow of the Holocaust and the afterglow of the creation of the state of Israel. Just a few years after the destruction of European Jewry, a shattered people had declared, in 1948, that the "ever-dying people" had made a miraculous new beginning. But, just as light remains a quality of matter even though blind people don't see it, neither the author of *Eichmann in Jerusalem: A Report on the Banality of Evil*[1] nor her acolytes could see the transcendent meaning in this heroic recovery.

Hannah Arendt's book first appeared in *New Yorker* articles of February and March before being published as a book in May. The English novelist George Eliot had predicted (in 1876) that some day, when the Jews were no longer a dispersed people, they would "have a defense, in the court of nations, [just] as the outraged Englishman or American" did. But not even the great sibyl could have prophesied that in the twentieth century "crimes against the Jewish people" would include the destruction of European Jewish civilization.

Arendt's book aroused a storm of controversy, primarily because it alleged that the Jews had cooperated significantly in their own destruction. Except among her most passionate disciples, it is now generally accepted that Arendt was woefully and willfully mistaken in this central assertion. In 1963 little serious historical research had been done on the subject of the *Judenrate*. But even to the meager historical material available Arendt paid little attention, preferring secondary sources that supported her accusation of Jewish collaboration. The abrasive effect of the book was increased by its original appearance in the *New Yorker*—discussion of mass murder alongside the ads for perfume, mink coats, and racing cars—and what Gershom Scholem (the great Jewish scholar who left Germany for Jewish Palestine in 1923) called its "heartless . . . sneering and malicious" tone toward Jewish leaders.

The rebuttal to Arendt came from Zionists like the journalist and poet Marie Syrkin, but also from non-Zionists like the socialist and literary critic Irving Howe. Howe had defended the Israeli capture of Eichmann in Argentina as a necessary moral act by the victims of Nazi Germany. He was outraged by the fact that Arendt's articles, which had brought the most serious charges against European Jews, their institutions, and their leaders, had been distributed to a mass audience unequipped to judge them critically, and had then been sealed shut against criticism in the *New Yorker* itself. The debate took place in the *Partisan Review*, although Arendt and her acolyte, the left-wing journalist Dwight Macdonald, did their best to stop editor William Phillips from printing critic Lionel Abel's attack on the book. (Abel, rejecting Arendt's condemnation of the Jewish Councils for "collaborating" with the Nazi killers, pointed out that in the Ukraine, where there was no Jewish Council to collaborate with the conquerors, the Nazis had nevertheless managed efficiently to destroy more than half a million Jews between November 1941 and June 1942.)

Dispute over the book, which also meant dispute over the state of Israel and over the ingrained intellectual tradition of blaming Jews for the violence unleashed against them, divided the New York intellectuals into opposing camps. Howe's magazine *Dissent* organized a public forum on the book early in the fall of 1963; it was attended by nearly five hundred people, who witnessed a debate between Arendt's detractors, Abel and Syrkin, and defenders like Holocaust historian

Raul Hilberg and sociologist Daniel Bell. Like the Dreyfus affair, the *Eichmann* controversy split families. Although Howe awarded the accolade for the "most judicious words in the whole debate" to Norman Podhoretz,[2] Podhoretz's wife Midge Decter later accused Howe of having arranged a "lynching" of Arendt and her book. Syrkin scoffed at the notion that the haughty Arendt could ever have been a defenseless lamb set upon by a frenzied mob. The symposium, she argued, was not a mere literary controversy about a book, but an examination of widely disseminated allegations of the Jews' complicity in their own destruction. Howe had performed notable service by involving a previously aloof sector of the Jewish intelligentsia in a consideration of the greatest crime of the century, and brought awareness of the catastrophe to a once indifferent group.

Certainly, the debate had brought awareness to Howe himself. Long after World War II ended, William Phillips recalled that Howe "was haunted by the question of why our intellectual community... had paid so little attention to the Holocaust in the early 1940s... why we had written and talked so little about the Holocaust at the time it was taking place." One may search the *Partisan Review* from 1937 through summer 1939 without finding mention of Hitler or Nazism. When writing his autobiography, Howe looked through the old issues of his own journal *Labor Action* to see how, or whether, he and his socialist comrades had responded to the Holocaust. He found the experience painful, and concluded that Trotskyists, including himself, were only the best of a bad lot of leftist sects, and that this inattention to the destruction of European Jewry was "a serious instance of moral failure on our part."

Nor was this their only moral failure. The leading New York intellectuals had shown appalling indifference not only to what had been endured by their European brethren but to what had been achieved by the Jews of Palestine. Events of biblical magnitude had occurred within a single decade: a few years after the destruction of European Jewry, the Jewish people had created the state of Israel. Like protagonists in a great tragedy, the Jewish people had imposed a pattern of meaning upon otherwise incomprehensible suffering. Winston Churchill, addressing Parliament in 1949, said, "The coming into being of a Jewish state in Palestine is an event in world history to be viewed in the perspective, not of a generation or a century, but in the perspective of a thousand, two thousand or even three thousand years."

Having averted their eyes from the destruction of European Jewry, the "first-rank" Jewish intellectuals now looked away from one of the most impressive assertions of the will to live that a martyred people has ever made. They had been immersed in the twists and turns of literary modernism, the fate of socialism in the USSR and the United States, and in themselves, especially their "alienation" from America and from Judaism and Jews. Indeed, they found their Jewish "identity" precisely in their alienation from Jewishness.

Looking back on this debacle many years later, novelist Saul Bellow admitted to fellow novelist Cynthia Ozick in a letter of 1987 that "it's perfectly true that 'Jewish Writers in America' . . . missed what should have been for them the central event of their time, the destruction of European Jewry. I can't say how our responsibility can be assessed. We . . . should have reckoned more fully, more deeply with it. Nobody in America seriously took this on and only a few Jews elsewhere (like Primo Levi) were able to comprehend it all. The Jews as a people reacted justly to it. So we have Israel, but in the matter of higher comprehension . . . there were no minds *fit* to comprehend. . . . All parties then are passing the buck and every honest conscience feels the disgrace of it. . . ." Four years after the *Eichmann in Jerusalem* controversy, the Six-Day War of June 1967 presented American Jewish intellectuals with a new challenge, one that, even more than Hannah Arendt had done, brought Holocaust "consciousness" to the fore. Gamal Abdel Nasser, declaring that "Israel's existence is itself an aggression," launched a war intended "to turn the Mediterranean red with Jewish blood." As in 1948, the Arabs lost the war on the battlefield, but they and their supporters threw their energies into rescinding its results. Having failed to destroy the Jewish state, they commenced an ideological onslaught against Zionism itself. Here, where the Jews were alleged to be adept, the defeated Arabs did much better. Having refused to admit a Jewish state into a region they proclaimed exclusively theirs, they accused the Jews of refusing to accept an Arab ("Palestinian") state; having launched several wars, countless terror attacks, and an international boycott, they accused Israel of aggression for defending itself. Having exploited Arab refugees they themselves had created and continued to exploit as human refuse, they blamed Israel for Palestinian homelessness.

In transforming their rhetoric from right to left, the Arabs made a calculated appeal to liberals, especially Jewish ones. The latter, as Ruth Wisse has pointed out, were now forced to choose between abandoning their faith in progress and enlightenment, and—once again—abandoning the Jews. Irving Howe saw what was coming. Even more contrite than

Bellow about his "moral failure" with respect to the Holocaust, he fore-saw the next great moral debacle of American Jewish intellectuals. As the verbal violence of the New Left turned into actual violence in the late sixties, his direst predictions of the "movement's" fate were being realized, especially by its Jewish cadre of liberal "explainers" of terror and their solemn attachment to the slogan (whose irony they missed entirely) *Tout comprendre, c'est tout pardonner.* By 1970 Howe found the treachery of the younger generation of Jewish intellectuals literally unspeakable: "Jewish boys and girls, children of the generation that saw Auschwitz, hate democratic Israel and celebrate as 'revolutionary' the Egyptian dictatorship; . . . a few go so far as to collect money for Al Fatah, which pledges to take Tel Aviv. About this, I cannot say more; it is simply too painful."

The late sixties and early seventies were also the years in which an earlier abandonment of the Jews—by American Jewry's most beloved and adored politician, FDR—had been made common knowledge among literate people by the books of David Wyman and Henry Feingold.[3] They revealed that, as Howe himself put it in *World of Our Fathers*, the record of the Roosevelt administration in admitting Jew-ish refugees had been "shameful," more stony-hearted than that of any European country. To this subject we shall return.

II: The Present

"Hegel remarks somewhere that all great world historic facts and personages appear, so to speak, twice. He forgot to add: the first time as tragedy, the second time as farce. . . ."

—Karl Marx, *Eighteenth Brumaire*

The questions that should have riveted the attention of American Jewish intellectuals during Hitler's twelve-year war against European Jewry had long ago been asked in the Bible: "Am I my brother's keeper?" (Gen. 4:9); and "And Moses said unto the children of Gad and the children of Reuben: 'Shall your brethren go to the war, and shall ye sit here?'" (Num. 32:6).

Generally, as we have seen, they were not the besetting questions. Has the belated recognition, by such formidable figures as Howe and Bellow, taught their successors among Diaspora Jewry's learned classes any lessons? Can they respond any more convincingly to Moses's ques-tion to "the children of Reuben" than their ancestors did during World War II? Have they learned, from the moral debacle of their intellectual predecessors, that survival must precede definition?

Many of those "Jewish boys and girls" whose hatred of Israel rendered the usually voluble Howe speechless would go on to become (some still are) well-established figures in journalism and academia, tigers of wrath who became insurrectionaries sitting in endowed university chairs, or editorializing in the *New York Times* or *New Yorker* or *New York Review of Books*. If ideological liberals became unsympathetic to the fate of the Jews in the Middle East because it contradicted their sanguine view of the world, the tenacity of the Arabs' rejection of Israel and their worldwide campaign to destroy Israel's moral image by "delegitimization" have brought a mass defection of Jewish liberals from Israel. They fall roughly into three categories.

First, in America as in England, there are the "ashamed Jews," American cousins of Howard Jacobson's fictional inventions. They are desperate to escape the negative role in which they are being cast by the alleged sins of Israel. Readers of spiteful broadsides against Israel by American Jewish intellectuals will notice the frequency with which these accusers mention the shame and embarrassment that overcome them at cocktail parties or in faculty lounges. Thus Berkeley history professor Martin Jay's notorious essay blaming Ariel Sharon for the rise of the new antisemitism begins as follows: "'No one since Hitler,' my dinner partner [another Jewish academic] heatedly contended, 'has done so much damage to the Jews as Ariel Sharon.' . . . This stunning accusation [was] made during a gracious faculty soiree in Princeton."[4]

Julien Benda, the French Jewish philosopher and novelist, once urged intellectuals of *all* countries "to tell your nations they are always in the wrong by the simple fact that they are nations. . . . Plotinus blushed at having a body. You should blush at having a nation." So far, however, only Jews have responded in substantial numbers to Benda's advice. The late Tony Judt, history professor at NYU, was perhaps the most famous victim of this newest entry in the nosology of social diseases. "Today," he wrote, "non-Israeli Jews feel themselves once again exposed to criticism and vulnerable to attack for things they didn't do. . . . The behavior of a self-described Jewish state affects the way everyone else looks at Jews. . . ."[5] Judt saw nothing "disproportionate" in recommending politicide—the end of Israel—as the cure for his insecurity. While Israelis worried about an Arab siege that is currently renewed every three years, Judt worried about embarrassment and how he looked to others.

Second, there are the Jews who nimbly turn their desire to advertise their own goodness by dissociating themselves from a people under attack into a mode of Jewish "identity." In 1942 the Hebrew writer

Haim Hazaz created (in his story "The Sermon") a literary character who declared that "when a man can no longer be a Jew, he becomes a Zionist." That motto has now been replaced by a new one: "When a man can no longer be a Jew, he becomes an *anti*-Zionist." Jewish intellectuals who cannot read the *alef-beys* discover their Jewish "identity" by denouncing Israel for its manifold sins, and call for the dismantling of the very state upon which their identity rests.

A third, perhaps more subtle form of identity creation via anti-Zionism is what might be called "the new Diasporism." It flourishes mainly among writers and scholars, including those in Jewish Studies who certainly can read the *alef-beys*. Ironically, this academic specialty, very much like Soviet Jewry's awareness of and yearning for Israel, came into being in large part because of the exuberance generated by Israel's victory in the Six-Day War. But now many of its practitioners bombard the university presses with manuscripts purporting to discover that the Jewish state, which most Europeans blame for the absence of world peace, should never have come into existence in the first place. They suggest or assert that "the [non-Zionist] roads not taken" would have brought (and may yet bring) a "new" Diaspora golden age. Some of them organize "academic conferences," which serve, in effect, as kangaroo courts, on "Alternative Histories within and beyond Zionism"; still others churn out articles or monographs or novels celebrating those roads not taken. A few even recommend a one-state solution or a no-state solution or (this from the tone-deaf literary critic George Steiner, like Judt an English product) "a final solution."

The strategy of the new Diasporists is at once timely and timeless. They dredge up from relative obscurity long-dead Jewish thinkers who opposed Zionism altogether or opposed political Zionism (a Jewish state) at the very time that their liberal and progressive colleagues are discovering that the nation-state is itself obsolete and that Israel is the most pernicious nation-state that exists or has ever existed. But in another sense they are ahistorical and disdainful of time and change because they write as if there were no difference between Jewish opposition to a conjectural Jewish state eighty or a hundred years ago and opposition to a living entity of eight million people (75% of them Jewish) under constant siege by genocidal Islamist fanatics boasting of their intention to "wipe Israel off the map." These are enemies who already have in place—in Iran, for example—the instruments for its destruction and willing accomplices (in Gaza and Lebanon) as well as ululating bystanders among Israel's neighbors.

Finally, we have the "Zionists against Israel," epitomized by an organization called J Street, which misses no opportunity to blacken Israel's reputation, and very few opportunities to encourage campaigns to delegitimize it, yet insists on calling itself "pro-Israel, pro-peace."

Its cofounder Daniel Levy calls Israel's creation "an act that went wrong." The organization cannot "pick a side" in the conflict between Israel and Hamas. It relentlessly castigates Israel's leaders for "harping" on Iran's nuclear ambitions and aspiration to obliterate Israel when they should be resolving "the Palestinian issue." It derides Israeli actions against terrorism as "escalation" or "cruel brutality," or—a favorite, of course—"disproportionate"; and it lobbies the American government to oppose the policies of the Israeli government. Funded by such billionaires as George Soros, who boasts of his strong ties to the Obama administration, and fancying itself a (Jewish) government-in-exile, J Street has a "Rabbinic Cabinet" whose members include supporters of Hamas's relentless bombing of Sderot and also Michael Lerner, the pioneering promoter of the "Palestinian cause" within the Jewish community. Typically, Lerner grants that Palestinian suicide bombings, lynchings, and pogroms may be "immoral," but Israel is not justified in protecting itself against them because it too is ethically impure. Besides, Israeli military responses to Arab terror are bad for the Jews, in Berkeley and other centers of prophetic morality: they cause "a frightening upsurge in anti-Semitism."[6] "Not since the days of the Communist Party," the sociologist Werner Cohn has written of J Street, "has there been a comparable spectacle of methodical disingenuousness in American political life."[7]

J Street is exceeded in misrepresentation and the pursuit of moral rectitude in disregard not just of reality but of danger (to Israelis, that is) only by Peter Beinart. If American Jewry is really divided between those who judge Judaism by the standards of the New York Times and those who judge the Times by the standards of Judaism, Beinart is the anointed philosopher king of the former group; indeed, it was the Times that published his book, called The Crisis of Zionism (2012), a title that recalls the equally nasty work of 1985 (The Tragedy of Zionism) by Bernard Avishai. Beinart is reported to have been assisted in this attempt to save Israel from itself (in Beinart's view, its sole mortal enemy)—and America from Israel—by advances from "progressive" Jews of several hundred thousand dollars. This stipend helped him to hire the twenty-four researchers whom he thanks for helping to assemble the 800 footnotes that adorn his prophetic denunciations of fallen Israel.

Believing that Judaism follows an arrow-straight course from Sinai to the left wing of the Democratic Party, Beinart contends that Zionism must do the same. Although second to none in sheer hatred for Israel as it actually exists, Beinart insists on calling himself a Zionist—but a "democratic" one, just like his grandmother. Indeed, "I wrote this book because of my grandmother." (The grandmothers of Jews who despise Israel must endure, in the next world as well as this one, a constant state of danger.) He supports (more explicitly than J Street) the sixty-five-year-old Arab economic boycott of Israel, but with a difference, intended to preserve the mask of the do-gooder, the fellow who confuses doing good with feeling good about what he is doing. He has urged, since at least 2010—in the *New York Review of Books*, the *New York Times*, and then his book—a "Zionist B.D.S. Movement," which would boycott, divest from, "sanction," only the so-called "oc-cupied" territories, the wicked "settlers" and those who deal with them. (The "selective" boycott requires boycotting feta cheese coming from cows in Judea but not companies—such as have been punished by the U.S. Treasury Department—that procure military equipment used by Hezbollah to murder Jews in Nahariya and Acco.)

Beinart is, however, very much against the blockade of Gaza from the sea, sporadically imposed by Israel to prevent the delivery of weapons, and for this reason considers the Hamas-ruled polity still "occupied" territory, many years after Israel's withdrawal. (It's true that Israel hasn't withdrawn totally. As of summer 2014, in the midst of Hamas's huge rocket bombardment of most of Israel and murderous infiltrations via the infamous Rachel Corrie Memorial Tunnels, Gaza was still receiving all of its gas and electricity, free of charge, from the ruthless Zionist oppressor.) Could Beinart possibly be unaware that Hamas goes to war against Israel every two or three years not be-cause it is "resisting" a (nonexistent) occupation or because it expects military triumph by firing thousands of rockets at Israeli civilians? Rather, it goes to war because it knows that Israeli counterattack to stop the rockets and destroy the tunnels will inevitably bring civilian Arab deaths and the ensuing propaganda triumph provided by liber-als (especially Jewish ones), for whom all Palestinian barbarities are proof of *Israeli* malevolence?

Beinart published his book at a midpoint in Barack Obama's presidential trajectory from "first black president" to "first Jewish presi-dent" (the title of chapter 5 of Beinart's book) to "first gay president," and so provided his hero with the second person of his triune divinity.

Lest anyone doubt Obama's credentials, Beinart conjures up a dream vision in which Rabbi Stephen Wise, meeting with Obama (and those Beinart deems today's woefully illiberal and unrepresentative Zionist leaders) in the Oval Office, pronounces the president the only genuine Zionist in the room, a liberal one just like himself. (The mind reels at the prospect of Stephen Wise cozying up to Obama favorites like the deranged Turkish antisemite Erdogan and the Egyptian leader of the Muslim Brotherhood, Morsi.)

The irony of Beinart's identification with Wise was pointed out by Sol Stern in a shrewd (and shrewdly entitled) piece called "Beinart the Unwise," but it merits elaboration. Wise was the most important American Jewish leader throughout FDR's long years in the White House. Although he wrote to a colleague in 1933 that "FDR has not lifted a finger on behalf of the Jews of Germany," he came to adore the man who was, after all, commander in chief of the war against Hitler. American Jews, he said, "rightly look up to [FDR], revere him, and love him. . . . No one would more deeply sorrow than I . . . if this feeling of Jewish homage . . . should be changed." Wise obsequiously (Jeremiah, with whom Beinart confuses himself, would have said idolatrously) referred to Roosevelt as "the all Highest." In his best-known "Dear Boss" letter to FDR (November 1942) about irrefutable reports of the mass murder of European Jewry, Wise apologized for impinging on the president's precious time ("I do not wish to add an atom to the awful burden which you are bearing with magic"), confessed that he had kept the terrible information secret and sworn other Jewish leaders to do so, and asked the president not for a rescue plan, but only "a word which may bring solace . . . to millions of Jews who mourn." In May 1944 Wise, together with Nahum Goldmann, actually urged FDR's State Department to deport the leaders of the Bergson Group,[8] by far the most effective force at work in America for the rescue of Europe's Jews. The reasoning of Wise and Goldmann was precisely the apologia Roosevelt used for not admitting Jewish refugees: Bergson activities (rallies, newspaper ads, rabbinical marches on Washington) would stir up the (conjectural) antisemitism of Americans.

By May 2012 Beinart, as a reward for his own sycophancy, was invited to the White House to "share" his views on how to renew the "peace process." (Michael Lerner, of whom Beinart—especially in his resort to language that turns Israelis into Nazis and Arabs into Jews[9]—is a more carefully barbered clone, had also, in 1993, been given entrée to the White House. But Lerner was supposed to serve the spiritual needs of

Mrs. Clinton rather than the political ones of her husband.) Beinart had become the reincarnation of the Stephen Wise of his dream vision, just as (in his view) Benjamin Netanyahu is the ideological reincarnation of his late father, Benzion Netanyahu. (Bibi's public endorsement of the idea of a Palestinian state, the very opposite of his father's views, was for Beinart merely typical Israeli subterfuge.)

The elder Netanyahu, let us recall, had become the preeminent historian of the Spanish Inquisition because he discerned the very truth constantly denied by Beinart: antisemitism is not the result of Jewish misbehavior but of the Jew-haters' panic. The elder Netanyahu was active in the aforementioned Bergson Group and also executive director of the Revisionists (New Zionist Organization of America), about whom Beinart regurgitates the fixed epithets that, as Orwell observed long ago, progressives reserve for people they don't like: "fascist" and "militarist." (Beinart is sublimely ignorant of the fact that Martin Buber used similar language about Labor Zionists.) But Benzion Netanyahu's greatest sin, in Beinart's eyes, must surely be that he went regularly to Washington with the express purpose of establishing ties with prominent figures in the *Republican* Party in order to promote the twin goals of rescue and the Jewish claim to Palestine. (It was due to such renegade efforts by Wise's Jewish opponents that in 1944 first the Republicans and then—in large part out of political necessity—FDR and the Democrats incorporated support of Israel into their presidential platforms. That is the reason why America remains, even now under a president in whose ostensibly warm heart there is always a cold spot for the Jews, Israel's sole reliable ally.)

Beinart gave Obama two copies of his book at their May meeting, and in return received Obama's encouragement to stand firm against his detractors (who by this time included even several "liberal" Zionists): "Hang in there," Beinart is reported to have been told by the grateful recipient of his adoration. His polemic brings us, full circle, back to the painful subject of American Jewry and the Holocaust, and also to a still more enduring theme: the need to choose between survival and definition. That need was uppermost in the mind of the great Revisionist Zionist Vladimir Jabotinsky (of whom Beinart knows almost nothing except cliché) when he wrote to his adversary Ben-Gurion in 1935 as follows: "I can vouch for there being a type of Zionist who doesn't care what kind of society our 'state' will have; I'm that person. If I were to know that the only way to a state was via socialism, or even that this would hasten it by a generation, I'd welcome it. More than that: give me a religiously Orthodox state in which I would be forced to eat gefillte fish all day long (but only if there were no other way) and I'll take it. More than that: make it a Yiddish-speaking state, which for me would mean the loss of all the magic in the thing—if there's no other way, I'll take that, too." But Jabotinsky died in 1940, and perhaps could not foresee that the choice of Palestine might require the surrender of all hope for rescuing European Jewry. Were Beinart and his battalion of research assistants to undertake serious research on the subject, they might be surprised to discover that the split between Wise and the Bergson Group over how to rescue European Jewry was not primarily one between left and right but between Zionists and rescuers; and in that struggle *his* man, Wise, was on the side of the Zionists. In 1962 the historian Lucy Dawidowicz wrote that "political Zionists" like Wise "gambled away [the] one chance to save the Jews" by emphasizing the Palestine issue instead of rescue in 1943–44. Samuel Merlin, although he was the cofounder with Menachem Begin of the Herut political party, emphasized that "Bergson once explained to Rabbi Stephen Wise, in a private conversation, that if the rabbi was trapped in a house that was on fire, his main concern would be how to get out alive, not how to get to the Waldorf Astoria."[10]

But there is a still more important issue here, one that brings us back to the confessions of regret by Saul Bellow and Irving Howe about their indifference to the destruction of European Jewry during the 1940s. Can Beinart possibly be ignorant of the fact that the record of the Roosevelt administration in helping to save or admit Jewish refugees was abominable? Perhaps—after all, the greatest deceivers are the self-deceivers. Since Beinart knows that in those occasional moments of modesty when Obama does not see himself as a second Lincoln, he imagines himself a second Franklin Roosevelt, Beinart must, if only at some subterranean level, sense that Roosevelt's abandonment of the Jews is being repeated by Obama's icy indifference to the plight of Israelis forced to live in what Conor O'Brien called a permanent state of siege. The reason why FDR could rebuff not only the Bergson Group but also Rabbi Wise was clearly defined by Howe in *The World of Our Fathers*: "The Jewish organizations lacked political leverage with the Roosevelt administration precisely because the American Jewish vote was so completely at the disposal of the president. Had they been able to threaten that, unless the government took more courageous steps to save the refugees, crucial swing votes in crucial states might be withdrawn, it is at least possible that they could have had some effect."[11] *Plus ça change, plus c'est la même chose.*

Notes

1. Adolf Eichmann, a leading organizer of the Nazi destruction of European Jewry, was captured by Israeli agents in Argentina in 1960 and brought to Jerusalem to stand trial.

2. The concluding words of Podhoretz's fierce attack on Arendt were these: "The Final Solution reveals nothing about the victims except that they were mortal beings and hopelessly vulnerable in their weakness. . . . The Nazis destroyed a third of the Jewish people. In the name of all that is humane, will the remnant never let up on itself?"

3. David Wyman, *The Abandonment of the Jews: America and the Holocaust, 1941–1945* (New York: Pantheon, 1985); Henry R. Feingold, *The Politics of Rescue: The Roosevelt Administration and the Holocaust* (New Brunswick, NJ: Rutgers University Press, 1970).

4. Martin Jay, "Ariel Sharon and the Rise of the New Anti-Semitism," *Salmagundi* (Winter–Spring 2003).

5. Tony Judt, "Israel: The Alternative," *New York Review of Books*, October 23, 2003.

6. *The Nation*, May 2002.

7. "J Street—The Gentle Façade and What's Behind It," FringeGroups.com, March 31, 2011.

8. Peter Bergson (a pseudonym for Hillel Kook) was a founding figure, with Menachem Begin, of the Irgun fighting force for Jewish independence in Palestine. But the outbreak of World War II convinced him that rescue of European Jewry was a still more urgent task, and he tried, often spectacularly, to raise awareness in America of the Jewish catastrophe. See David S. Wyman and Rafael Medoff, *A Race against Death: Peter Bergson, America, and the Holocaust* (New York: The New Press, 2002); Sonya S. Wentling and Rafael Medoff, *Herbert Hoover and the Jews: The Origins of the "Jewish Vote" and Bipartisan Support for Israel* (Washington, DC: Wyman Institute, 2012); Samuel Merlin, *Millions of Jews to Rescue*, ed. Rafael Medoff (Washington, DC: Wyman Institute, 2012).

9. In May 2014, for example, Beinart (now working for *Ha'aretz*) "tweeted" to his 24,000 loyal readers that Jewish "settlers" had perpetrated a "Lag B'Omer pogrom" by burning an Arab orchard of olive trees. In fact, there was no such event, and *Ha'aretz* had to print a retraction. But Beinart's use of that word "pogrom" was more noteworthy than the retraction.

10. Merlin, *Millions of Jews*, 157.

11. *The World of Our Fathers* (New York: Harcourt Brace Jovanovich, 1976), 394.

7

The Holocaust . . . and Me
(1990)

In Piotr Rawicz's powerful novel *Blood from the Sky*, the narrator-protagonist, Boris, is urged to take up "the vocation to be witness" to the murder of the Jewish people of Europe. But when, having survived the carnage, he turns to the task of testimony, he finds that the "I" who lived in the town and endured prison and torture hardly exists in the man who puts pen to paper. "When a whirlwind comes along," he cynically concludes, "one must make the most of it, exploit it, start writing at once, lying at once." Indeed, after the Holocaust, "the 'literary manner' is an obscenity by definition."

The difficulty that even Holocaust survivors face in testifying to, or representing in a literary imitation, an unprecedented abomination does not seem to have troubled more than a few of the twenty-seven contributors to David Rosenberg's egregiously titled *Testimony: Contemporary Writers Make the Holocaust Personal*.[1] This book testifies to nothing so much as Rawicz's acrid definition of the literature that tries to "personalize" the Holocaust as "the art, occasionally remunerative, of rummaging in vomit." Indeed, one uneasy contributor (Gordon Lish) confesses, "Yes, I am being paid for this. . . . If it looks as if anyone is possibly ashamed of this, then just chalk it up to strictly looks" (415). The title *Testimony*, in its pretentious appropriation of an idea that has acquired historical and moral resonance for Jews, was offensive enough when I began reading the unrevised proofs of the book in unadorned paper covers. But only when the finished product arrived, lavishly illustrated on dust jacket, title page, and chapter openers, with details from *Curtain for the Torah Ark* (Italy, 1643–44), did the full horror of the book's blasphemous vulgarity reveal itself.[2]

The Torah ark curtain proclaims that this testimony has an almost sacred quality, intended to call to mind Exodus 25:16: "And thou shalt put into the ark the testimony which I shall give thee." But what we actually find in this five-hundred-page monument to egoism is (with a few exceptions) much closer to the profane than to the sacred, much more akin to the advertiser who offers "to personalize your paper towels" than to the moral heroism of which Hannah Arendt wrote when she referred to the testimony of "one man [who] will always be left alive to tell the story." The common reader's most frequent reaction to the responses given by Rosenberg's twenty-seven contributors to his questions about how their lives and writing careers have been shaped by the Holocaust will be: "Who cares?" Who cares about the failed marriages of Anne Roiphe or Alfred Kazin, or the Ashanti circumcision of Leslie Fiedler's grandson? Who cares that Leonard Michaels's "life was a mess" (ll) when he heard Arendt give a lecture, or that Daphne Merkin was hospitalized at age eight for psychiatric observation because she thought of her father (a German Jew) as "a Nazi manqué" (18), and of her mother as Ilse Koch? Who cares that "God became the God of the Holocaust" for Anne Roiphe in "the year of my puberty" (135), or that she thinks she married a non-Jew because of the Holocaust? Who cares that Fiedler resents people who "wrongly" assume that he is a Jew (which he is)?

Worse still than the mawkish, self-pitying, licentious equations between their Lilliputian "personal" disturbances and the torture and murder of European Jewry are the "ideas" of these literary scribblers. Here ignorance and arrogance are in full flower. Most exploded fictions about the Holocaust—ranging from the notion that not only Jews but also Poles, Communists, and homosexuals were chosen by the Nazis for total annihilation, to the imbecilic description (by Phillip Lopate) of the majority of the Jewish victims as "religious peasants" (293), to the tale about body fat being reduced into soap—are dredged up repeatedly, apparently to the satisfaction of the book's editor. Contempt for Israel is rife among most of these writers; and, despite the fact that Israel is the only country in the world whose neighbors (with the highly unpredictable exception of Egypt) have for many decades denied its right to exist, many of Rosenberg's testifiers see another Holocaust in prospect for virtually every group except the Jews. Several "worry" about Latin America or the omnipresent "Palestinians"; and E. M. Broner's uncurbed benevolence embraces nothing less than "the earth . . . in mortal danger" (279). Conjectural speculation about how Zionism *might* "grow into a fanatical passion" (thus Geoffrey Hartman, [431]) like the nationalism that laid waste European Jewry is more in evidence than simple respect for the Jews who actually died. One hopes that

Daphne Merkin's tongue will cling to the roof of her mouth next time she feels the itch to mock "overweight Jewish women standing before open pits, covering their pubes with their hands" (18).

Rosenberg reports that the working title for *Testimony* was *Sheltered Lives*. Alan Lelchuk, in one of the few good essays in the book, modestly explains what this means: "Over here, in America, a small Jewish boy was following the Dodgers and listening to 'The Shadow' and 'The Green Hornet' and playing boxball on the sidewalk, while, over there, in Europe, the game was the killing of Jews. Such was history" (254). The book's most riveting (and learned) essay, by Susanne Schlotelburg, rejects *Testimony*'s premise by arguing that "to ensure remembrance the Holocaust would have to be made transpersonal rather than personal," and that those who are not bound by *akedah* or *brith* are no more likely to remember the Holocaust than the Crusades (353). Most of the book's contributors, however, remain just as sheltered from the Holocaust now as their predecessors (and sometimes they themselves) were in the 1940s. Thus Leslie Fiedler, like some curious insect preserved in amber from the pre-Holocaust (or pre-Dreyfus) period, holds forth about how his "love of all humanity, including those who have long persecuted us," leads him to urge Jews "to cease to exist in their chosenness for the sake of a united mankind" (229). It never occurs to Fiedler that, as Emil Fackenheim has written, after the Holocaust a commitment to Jewish survival is precisely "a testimony to life against death *on behalf of all mankind.*"[3]

Outdoing even Fiedler in his mercifulness toward "those who have long persecuted us" and (no easy task) far outdoing all other contributors in the gross, the flagrant, the blatant, is the tooth-baring Phillip Lopate. Lopate seethes with hatred and rage—not against the Nazis (in fact, he speculates on the "youthful idealism" of the SS and praises President Reagan's laying a wreath on the SS tombs at Bitburg as a gesture of "old-fashioned Homeric nobility" [294]), but against the Jews. These include the middle-class victims, "lined up in their fedoras and overcoats" (293); his own mother, who was "erotically excited" by blue numbers on the arms of survivors; and those he derides as "Holocaustians" (287), including Yehuda Bauer, Elie Wiesel, and the late Lucy Dawidowicz.

Too obtuse to understand that the uniqueness of the Holocaust consists neither in the number of Jews killed nor in the degree of individual suffering but in the fact that Hitler's was a war against the Jews, that Jews occupied the central place in his mental universe, that

Jews alone were singled out for total destruction, and that European Jewish civilization *was* totally destroyed, Lopate keeps flailing away at Jewish "chauvinism" (299), Jewish "ethnic muscle-flexing" (296), Jewish "tribal smugness," Jewish "pushiness" (307), and Jewish lack of compassion "for the other victimized peoples of this century" (300). He recommends as ultimate wisdom on memorializing the victims of the Holocaust a passage from Avishai Margalit's "brilliant essay" (298) in the *New York Review of Books*, on "The Kitsch of Israel." In this passage Margalit heaped scorn on the "children's room" at Yad Vashem with its "tape-recorded voices of children crying out in Yiddish, 'Mame, Tate.'" Any visitor to Yad Vashem knows that there is no "children's room" or taped children's voices there. There is a memorial to the murdered children and a tape-recorded voice that reads their names. Apparently, Lopate's "aesthetic" sense of the fitness of things is more offended by Jewish mourning than by Jewish lying.

Lopate's description of the very word *holocaust* as a Jewish conspiracy in which "one ethnic group tries to compel the rest of the world" to follow its political program, his voracious munching on the "grain of truth" in "the more moderate revisionist historians" (294), and his allegation that Jews have been able to "own the Holocaust" only because of political clout ("There are many more Jews in the United States than there are Ibos or Bengalis" [293]) bring him perilously close to the position of the neo-Nazis. "Before I give the wrong impression," he nervously announces, "let me interject that I am not one of those revisionist nuts who deny that the Nazis . . . exterminated millions of Jews" (286). Lopate might have added that, despite appearances to the contrary, his essay could hardly be called antisemitic since it originally appeared in a Jewish magazine called *Tikkun*, of which, in fact, he was then the literary editor.

The reason why so many of the essays in this volume are egocentric, mean-spirited, and vulgar is not far to seek. Most of these American Jewish writers are people for whom the post-Enlightenment emancipation formula—"Be a man in the street and a Jew in your tent"—seems perfectly natural. Having accepted the disfiguring privatization of Jewish self-definition, they feel no shame in "making personal" a loss that was sustained by the whole Jewish people. When the Yiddish poet Jacob Glatstein, who was also safe in America while European Jewry was being murdered, wrote that "just as we all stood together / at the giving of the Torah, / so did we all die together at Lublin," he immersed himself in the vast ocean of Jewish civilization. When the contributors to *Testimony* speculate about how the Holocaust has affected their sex life or their politics, they are navigating an enclosed basin.

When first reading this wretched book, I learned of the death of Dorothea Krook, Israel's most distinguished literary critic, winner of the Israel Prize for her *Elements of Tragedy*, and one of the country's great, vibrant characters. Doris (as her friends called her) also had a "personal" relation to the Holocaust, but it was expressed in the desire to do something for the Jewish people rather than to contemplate herself. I remember how, many years ago, she came to my office in the Tel Aviv English Department carrying a large shopping bag that held a large manuscript. "I want," she said, "to talk about something *not* literary, something that has preyed on my mind ever since the end of the Second World War." This "something" was the question: "What can *I* do to redeem those who were killed in Europe, to heal this terrible wound in our people?" Doris had already done more in this direction than all the contributors to *Testimony*: she had resigned her position at Cambridge University to go on *aliyah* to Israel in 1960. But she had long brooded over and, in her last years, immersed herself in a scheme (elaborately articulated in the manuscript) for a "great *aliyah*" whose motive power would be an appeal to young Jews in America to secure the Jewish future by viewing themselves as "replacements" for those murdered in Europe.

One has only to read *Testimony* to see how wildly Doris overestimated the idealism of American Jewry, and how quixotic, even mad, her scheme was. Yet it is worth remembering that it was from a still more mad and quixotic scheme that Herzl's Jewish state arose—and that from the egocentric contemplation of Jewish navels nothing has, can, or will come.

Notes

1. *Testimony: Contemporary Writers Make the Holocaust Personal* (New York: Random House, 1989). Subsequent references to this work will be cited in parentheses in the text.
2. In fairness, it should be noted that, in one particular, the book's final version is an improvement on the bound proofs. The latter contain Phillip Lopate's most memorable words about the Holocaust: "I am deeply sorry it happened." Although this classic utterance would have given new meaning to the idea of the banality of evil, Rosenberg and Lopate chose to sacrifice it in the final version of the book.
3. Emil L. Fackenheim, *The Jewish Return into History* (New York: Schocken Books, 1978), 54.

8

Noam Chomsky and Holocaust Denial (1993)

"I see no antisemitic implications in the denial of the existence of gas chambers or even in denial of the Holocaust."

—Noam Chomsky

In 1980 Noam Chomsky discovered Robert Faurisson, a right-wing antisemite and onetime lecturer in literature at the University of Lyon 2, whose catalog of 1978 described him (with comic solemnity) as specializing in "investigation of meaning and counter-meaning, of the true and the false." His guiding dogma is that "Hitler never ordered (nor permitted) that someone be killed because of race or religion." If the Nazis built gas chambers, it was for gassing lice. After all, did not Himmler himself say that "it is the same with antisemitism as with delousing"? One of his central premises is that the only witnesses to the Holocaust are Jews, and that Jewish witnesses are liars—because they are Jews. This opinion did not prevent him from being adorned by a faction of the French ultra-left with the title of "the Jew," that is, "a man alone,"[1] a label that fits him almost as well as "a sort of apolitical liberal," which is the sage Chomsky's description of this antisemite.[2] The lie and "swindle" about gas chambers and genocide, Faurisson alleged, originate with the "Zionists" and victimize primarily "the Germans and Palestinians."

Faurisson has vaulted to fame not so much through his jejune publications as through his good fortune in finding a powerful friend to defend him from his persecutors, that other great ally of the "Palestinians," Noam Chomsky, who came to the defense of Faurisson after his university classes had been suspended[3] and he had been brought into

59

court in June 1981 for defamations of Holocaust witnesses and scholars of the Holocaust. Chomsky promoted (and placed his name at the head of) a petition supporting Faurisson's "just right of academic freedom" and worshipfully identifying him as someone who had been "conducting extensive historical research into the 'Holocaust' question" and was harassed as soon as "he began making his *findings* public"[4] (emphasis added). As Pierre Vidal-Naquet has remarked, "what is scandalous about the petition is that it never raises the question of whether what Faurisson is saying is true or false, that it even presents his conclusions or 'findings' as the result of a historical investigation, one, that is, in quest of the truth. To be sure, it may be argued that every man has a right to lies and falsehood. . . . But the right that the forger demands should not be conceded to him in the name of truth."[5]

Although Deborah Lipstadt in her book *Denying the Holocaust*[6] assigns considerable blame to Chomsky's "Voltairean" defense of the Nazis' free speech for their ability to penetrate the campuses, she pays insufficient attention to its still darker implications. These were captured succinctly by Nadine Fresco when she commented on the pregnancy of the fact that Chomsky selects as his model the Enlightenment bigot who in 1745 said of the Jews, "You will not find in them anything but an ignorant and barbarous people who have for a long time combined the most sordid avarice with the most detestable superstition," and then added the paradoxical coda: "One should not, however, burn them."[7] Neither has Lipstadt (perhaps because she lacks training in abnormal psychology) tried to track Chomsky down the winding path whereby he moved deeper and deeper into the revisionist morass, arguing, first, that denial of the Holocaust is no evidence of antisemitism; second, that anti-Zionism too implies no presumption of antisemitism; and third, in a truly spectacular example of *tu quoque* that he concocted in 1991, that anyone who says that the Jews alone were singled out by Hitler for total annihilation is involved in "pro-Nazi apologetics" (presumably because a genuine anti-Nazi would insist—erroneously—that Hitler wanted to annihilate *all* identifiable groups except ethnic Germans).[8]

At times Chomsky has given the impression that immaculate agnosticism moves him to defend the deniers. In *Liberation* (December 23, 1980) he wrote that "I don't know enough about [Faurisson's] work to determine if what he is claiming is accurate or not." In *Le Matin* (January 19, 1981) the newly tolerant linguist wrote that "we don't want people to have religious or dogmatic beliefs about the existence of the Holocaust." But we may conjecture that even though he does not directly endorse the claims of Faurisson and the other cranks, he wishes them well in their endeavor; for he believes that to undermine belief in the Holocaust is to undermine belief in the legitimacy of the state of Israel, which many people suppose (albeit mistakenly) to have come into existence because of Western bad conscience over what was done to the Jews in World War II. Chomsky would feel no compunction about joining "right-wing" forces to achieve the great desideratum of delegitimizing the Jewish state.

Chomsky surely recognizes that the underlying motive of the Holocaust deniers, like that of much of his own political labor, is hatred of the state of Israel. Indeed, the crucial place of Israel in the demonology of the deniers is the most relentlessly pursued theme of Lipstadt's book, and articles denying the Holocaust have long been a staple of PLO publications. Almost without exception the deniers claim that the Jews invented the "legend" of the Holocaust because they wanted license from the world to "displace" the poor Palestinians and establish the Jewish state, and they wanted the helpless, defeated Germans to finance the operation. Of course, the neo-Nazis ignore the fact that most reparations money was paid to individuals, and constantly accuse Israel of exaggerating the number of Jews killed so it could receive more German money. In fact, as Lipstadt remarks, since the money Israel did receive was based on the cost of resettling *survivors*, it would have been in Israel's interest to claim that fewer than six million had been killed and that more had managed to reach Israel. Austen App, for example, accused the "Talmudists" of using "the six million swindle to blackmail West Germany into 'atoning' with the twenty billion dollars of indemnities to Israel" (Lipstadt, 95). (The sum Germany paid to the state of Israel was $110 million.)

Denying the Holocaust is a book that was undertaken with great reluctance, for its author was keenly aware that for the deniers there is no such thing as unfavorable publicity. She began as "an ardent advocate of ignoring them" but after examining their activities closely decided that they will not retreat unless aggressively beaten back. Without according them legitimacy by "debating" them, either in the TV talk shows that have incessantly invited her to do so or in the book itself, Lipstadt has, in her scholarly and dispassionate exposé of the deniers' political program, fake scholarship, and fraudulent methods, exploded every one of their claims. Whether her tenacious effort will explode the movement itself remains to be seen. "The wicked," says Isaiah (57:20), "are like the troubled sea; / For it cannot rest, / And its waters cast up mire and dirt."

Notes

1. Nadine Fresco, "The Denial of the Dead: The Faurisson Affair—and Noam Chomsky," *Dissent* 28 (Fall 1981): 469.

2. Chomsky, preface to Robert Faurisson, *Mémoire en défense: contre ceux qui m'accusent de falsifier l'Histoire; La question des chambres à gaz* (Paris: La Vieille Taupe, 1980), xiv–xv.

3. His right to teach was not withdrawn, and his request to teach correspondence courses was approved.

4. The petition is quoted in full in Werner Cohn, *The Hidden Alliances of Noam Chomsky* (New York: Americans for a Safe Israel, 1988), 6.

5. Pierre Vidal-Naquet, *Assassins of Memory* (New York: Columbia University Press, 1992), 58.

6. Deborah Lipstadt, *Denying the Holocaust: The Growing Assault on Truth and Memory* (New York: The Free Press, 1993). Subsequent references to this book appear in parentheses in the text.

7. See the entry "Juif" in Voltaire's *Dictionnaire Philosophique*.

8. Electronic mail USENET network (soc.culture.Jewish newsgroup), August 19 and September 12, 1991.

9

Antisemitism Denial: The Berkeley School (2006)

"I have to be here. Berkeley is the center of the world-historical spirit."
—Michael Lerner[1]

1. Judith Butler: "No, It's Not Antisemitic"

The intense hostility to Israel evinced by several prominent Jewish professors at the Berkeley branch of University of California (the names Daniel Boyarin, Judith Butler, Chana Kronfeld, and Martin Jay spring quickly to mind) has given rise to a whole school of "UC Berkeley" apologetics that might be called "No, it's not antisemitic." The most highly publicized instance of these apologias is Judith Butler's debate with Harvard president Lawrence Summers after he had (in September 2002) deplored the upsurge of antisemitism around the globe, but with special attention to the faculty-initiated petitions at Harvard and other universities calling for them "to single out Israel among all nations as the lone country where it is inappropriate for any part of the university endowment to be invested."[2]

Butler perfunctorily assented to Summers's recommendation that—as she artfully restated it—"every progressive person ought to challenge anti-semitism vigorously," but seemed incapable either of recognizing it in such (to her) mild "public criticisms" as economic warfare against the Jewish state or calls for its dismantling or assaults on Zionism itself or opposing any effort Israel might make to defend against suicide bombers. Indeed, she saw no difference between Jews intentionally murdered by suicide bombers and Arabs accidentally killed by Israeli efforts to repel people bent on murdering them. Above all, she presented herself as offering Jews a salutary warning against

63

crying wolf: "If the charge of anti-semitism is used to defend Israel at all costs, then its power when used against those who do discriminate against Jews—who do violence to synagogues in Europe [synagogues and seders in Israel are not mentioned], wave Nazi flags or support anti-semitic organizations—is radically diluted."[3]

Butler called it wildly improbable that somebody examining the divestment petitions signed by herself and her co-conspirators might take them (as hundreds on her own campus already had) as condoning antisemitism. "We are asked to conjure a listener who attributes an intention to the speaker: so-and-so has made a public statement against the Israeli occupation, and this must mean that so-and-so hates Jews or is willing to fuel those who do." But Summers was perfectly correct in stating that one need not "hate Jews" in order to perform actions or utter words that are "antisemitic in their effect if not their intent." Having failed to recognize the importance of "intention" in different kinds of violence, she now got it wrong in the opposite way when considering verbal action.

Let us take a well-known case: when Dickens wrote *Oliver Twist*, he harbored no hatred of Jews and had no conscious intention to harm them. Indeed, he said of Fagin that "he's such an out and outer I don't know what to make of him." The reason for Dickens's puzzlement was that, in an important sense, he did not indeed "make" Fagin, and therefore didn't know what to make *of* him. Fagin was ready-made for Dickens by the collective folklore of Christendom, which had for centuries fixed the Jew in the role of Christ-killer, surrogate of Satan, inheritor of Judas, thief, fence, corrupter of the young—to which list of attributes Butler and her friends would now add "Zionist imperialist and occupier." Has *Oliver Twist* been antisemitic in its effect? Of course—or does Butler think that it is for their interest in Sikes and Nancy and the plight of the homeless in Victorian England that Arab publishers have long kept cheap paperback translations of the book in print?

2. Making the Case For Jew-Hatred: Martin Jay Explains How Jews Cause Antisemitism

"There is a great temptation to explain away the intrinsically incredible by means of liberal rationalizations. In each one of us, there lurks such a liberal, wheedling us with the voice of common sense."

—Hannah Arendt[4]

The academic boycotters of Israeli universities and the professorial advocates of suicide bombing of Israeli citizens are in the front lines of the defense of terror, which is the very essence of Palestinian nationalism.[5] But they themselves are supported by a rearguard of fellow travelers, a far more numerous academic group whose defining characteristic is not fanaticism but time-serving timorousness. In the thirties "fellow travelers" usually referred to the intellectual friends of Communism (well analyzed in David Caute's book on the subject[6]), although Hitler competed with Stalin in attracting people from America and Britain who never actually joined the Nazi or Communist parties but served their purposes in the conviction that they were engaged (at a safe distance) in a noble cause. At the moment, as Martin Peretz has pointed out,[7] the favorite cause of peregrinating political tourists is the Palestinian movement; and the reason why fellow travelers favor this most barbaric of all movements of "national liberation" is that its adversaries are Jews, always a tempting target because of their ridiculously small numbers (currently, 997 out of every 1,000 people in the world are *not* Jews) and their enormous image (as Christ-killers, corrupters of the young, thieves, agents of Satan, beneficiaries of Judas, devils dancing around the cross, Zionist imperialists).

As a representative example of the academic fellow traveler in the ongoing campaign to depict Israel as the center of the world's evil and make it ideologically vulnerable to terror, take the case of Martin Jay, a professor of history at University of California, Berkeley and author of books about the Frankfurt school in Germany and "ocularcentric discourse" in France. In the winter–spring 2003 issue of *Salmagundi*, a quarterly journal of the social sciences and humanities, Jay argues, in an essay entitled "Ariel Sharon and the Rise of the New Anti-Semitism,"[8] that Jews themselves, primarily Sharon and the "fanatic settlers" (22) but also the American Jews who question the infallibility of the *New York Times* and National Public Radio or protest the antics of tenured guerrillas on the campuses, are "causing" the "new" antisemitism. Jay, unlike such people as Edward Said (of whom he writes with oily sycophancy), does not deny the existence of a resurgent antisemitism, although his examples of its manifestations are vandalized synagogues and cemeteries, "tipping over a tombstone in a graveyard in Marseilles or burning torahs in a temple on Long Island [as] payback for *atrocities* [my emphasis] committed by Israeli settlers" (14); such unpleasant words as stabbings, shootings, murder—all of which have been unleashed against Jews in Europe as well as Israel—are not part of Jay's vocabulary. But his main interest is in proposing that the Jews are themselves the cause of the aggression against them. "The actions of contemporary Jews," Jay alleges, "are somehow connected with the

65

upsurge of anti-Semitism around the globe" (21), and it would be foolish to suppose that "the victims are in no way involved in unleashing
the animosities they suffer" (17).

Although Jay's main concern is the (supposedly) "new" antisemitism, his heavy reliance on the thesis and even the title of Albert Lindemann's unsavory and deviously polemical book *Esau's Tears: Modern
Anti-Semitism and the Rise of the Jews* (1998) suggests that he believes
political antisemitism, from its inception in the nineteenth century,
has been in large part the responsibility of the Jews themselves.
Lindemann's book argued not merely that Jews had "social interactions" (a favorite euphemism of Jay's) with their persecutors but were
responsible for the hatreds that eventually consumed them in Europe;
antisemitism was, wherever and whenever it flared up, a response to
Jewish misbehavior. According to Lindemann, the Romanians had
been subjected to "mean-spirited denigration" of their country by
Jews, and so it was reasonable for Romania's elite to conclude that
"making life difficult" for the country's Jewish inhabitants, "legally or
otherwise," was a "justifiable policy." His abstruse research into Russian
history also revealed to him that whatever antisemitism existed there
was "hardly a hatred without palpable or understandable cause." The
1903 Kishinev pogrom, Lindemann grudgingly admitted, did occur but
was a relatively minor affair in numbers killed and wounded, which
the Jews, with typical "hyperbole and mendacity," exaggerated in order
to attract sympathy and money; it was a major affair only because it
revealed "a rising Jewish combativeness." (As for the *Protocols of the
Elders of Zion*, Lindemann apparently never heard of it, for it goes
unmentioned in his nearly fifty pages on Russia.) In Germany Jews
(especially the historian Heinrich Graetz) were guilty of a "steady
stream of insults and withering criticism . . . directed at Germans";
by contrast, Hitler (who published *Mein Kampf* in 1925–27) was a
"moderate" on the Jewish question prior to the mid-1930s; besides,
"nearly everywhere Hitler looked at the end of the war, there were
Jews who corresponded to anti-Semitic imagery." In addition to being
degenerate, ugly, dirty, tribalist, racist, crooked, and sexually immoral,
the Jews, as depicted by Lindemann, further infuriated their gentile
neighbors by speaking Yiddish: "a nasal, whining, and crippled ghetto
tongue."[9]

Although Jay is by no means in full agreement with Lindemann's
thesis (as he is with that of an even cruder polemic by Paul Breines
called *Tough Jews*[10]), he is intensely grateful to this courageous pioneer

66

for breaking a "taboo" (18) on the "difficult question about the Jewish role in causing anti-Semitism," for putting it "on the table" (21). (Readers familiar with this dismal topic will be disappointed to learn that neither Lindemann nor his admirer Jay is able to explain the "Jewish role" in causing the belief, widespread among Christian theologians from St. Augustine through the seventeenth century, that Jewish males menstruate.) This is a remarkable statement to come from a historian. Washington Irving's Rip van Winkle lost touch with history for twenty years while he slept; Jay's dogmatic slumber seems to have lasted thirty-six years, since 1967, when the brief post–World War II relaxation of antisemitism came to an end.

A brief history lesson is in order here. At the end of the Second World War, old-fashioned antisemites grudgingly recognized that the Holocaust had given antisemitism a bad name, that perhaps the time was right for a temporary respite in the ideological war against the Jews. But in 1967 the Jews in Israel had the misfortune to win the war that was unleashed against them by Gamal Nasser, who had proclaimed—in a locution very much akin to Jay's style of reasoning—that "Israel's existence is itself an aggression." After their defeat the Arabs reversed their rhetoric from "right" to "left," deemphasizing their ambition to "turn the Mediterranean red with Jewish blood" and instead blaming "the Middle East conflict" on the Jews themselves for denying the *Palestinians* a state (something that, of course, the Arabs could have given them any time during the nineteen years that they were entirely in control of the disputed territories of "the West Bank"). Since that time what Jay calls the "difficult question about the Jewish role in causing anti-Semitism" has not only been "on the table"; it has provided a royal feast for such heavy feeders as Alexander Cockburn, Desmond Tutu, Michael Lerner, the aforementioned Said, Patrick Buchanan, Noam Chomsky, most of the Israeli left, and scores (if not hundreds) of other scribblers. Indeed, the *New York Times*, which during World War II did its best to conceal the fact that Jews were being murdered en masse, now admits they *are* being murdered, but blames them for, in Jay-speak, "unleashing the animosities they suffer."

The particular form given by nearly all these forerunners of Lindemann is, of course, blatant reversal of cause and effect in taking for granted that it is Israeli occupation that leads to Arab hatred and aggression, when every normally attentive sixth grader knows that it is Arab hatred and aggression that lead (as they have always done from 1967 to 2002) to Israeli occupation. Jay is (characteristically) very fierce not with Lindemann for regurgitating every antisemitic slander dredged up from the bad dreams of Christendom, but with Lindemann's "overheated" (18) critics (in *Commentary*, in the *American Historical Review*, in *Midstream*). In the same manner, his outrage about suicide bombings is not against the bombers or their instructors and financiers but against "American Jewish panic" (23) and "Israeli toughness" (23) in reacting to them and so perpetuating (no cliché is too stale and stupid for Jay) "the spiral of violence" (23).

Just as Jay insinuates some mild criticism of Lindemann, he also "qualifies" every now and then his insistence that the Jews themselves are to blame for antisemitism, but always in a way that only serves to make his core argument all the more gross and flagrant. "Acknowledging this fact [that the Jewish victims are 'involved in unleashing' hatred of themselves] is not 'blaming the victim,' an overly simple formula that prevents asking hard and sometimes awkward questions, but rather understanding that social interactions are never as neat as moral oppo-sitions of good and evil" (17). Like most liberals, Jay cannot credit the full evil of the world. "In the case of the Arab war against the Jewish state," Ruth Wisse has observed, "obscuring Arab intentions requires identifying Jews as the cause of the conflict. The notion of Jewish responsibility for Arab rejectionism is almost irresistibly attractive to liberals, because the truth otherwise seems so bleak."[11] Although Jay tries to twist Hannah Arendt's well-known criticism of Sartre's foolish argument that the Jews survived in exile thanks to gentile persecu-tion into an endorsement of his own foolish argument about Jewish *responsibility* for that persecution, he is himself a classic case of what Arendt called the wheedling voice of "common sense" that lurks inside every liberal, explaining away the "intrinsically incredible,"[12] such as the fact that a people would choose to define itself by its dedication to the destruction of another people.

For the benefit of Jay (and others) in bondage to the liberal dogma that "social interactions are never as neat as moral oppositions of good and evil," and at the risk of violating decorum, I should like here to quote from the description by a physicist (Dr. Pekka Sinervo of the University of Toronto) of what happens when a conventional bomb is exploded in a contained space, such as a city bus traveling through downtown Jerusalem: "A person sitting nearby would feel, momentarily, a shock wave slamming into his or her body, with an 'overpressure' of 300,000 pounds. Such a blast would crush the chest, rupture liver, spleen, heart and lungs, melt eyes, pull organs away from surrounding tissue, separate hands from arms and feet from legs. Bodies would fly through the air or be impaled on the jagged edges of crumpled metal and broken glass."[13] These are among the little "animosities," the "social interactions," that Martin Jay says Israelis, including (one assumes) the schoolchildren who usually fill these buses, have brought upon themselves.

Jay does take note of the suicide bombers, brainwashed teenage Arab versions of the Hitler Youth, by administering a little slap on the wrist to tearful Esau: "To be fair, the Palestinian leadership that encourages or winks at suicide bombers shows no less counter-productive stupidity [than Sharon taking action *against* suicide bombers]" (23). (The flabby syntax matches the fatuous moral equation.) Thus does Jay's labored distinction between "causation" and "legitimation" (17), or between blaming the Jewish victims and making them responsible for antisemitic aggression, turn out to be a distinction without a difference. "*Tout comprendre,*" as the French say, "*c'est tout pardonner.*"

But pointing out Jay's shoddy history, Orwellian logic, and addiction to worn-out clichés about settlements and "occupied territories" does not quite bring us to the quick of this ulcer. Matthew Arnold used to say that there is such a thing as conscience in intellectual affairs. An examination of the tainted character of Jay's documentation, his "evidence," reveals an intellectual conscience almost totally atrophied; for there is hardly a single reference in the essay to recent events in Intifada II (the Oslo War, that is) or the many responses to it that is not unreliable, deceptive, false.

The essay starts with a reference to the "occupation of Jenin" (12), which always lurks in the background of Jay's ominous albeit vague allusions to Sharon's "heavy-handed" policies and actions (23) and "bulldozer mentality" (22). The April 2002 reoccupation of Jenin infuriated both the academic Israel-haters alluded to above (their boycott of Israeli universities and research institutes, mainly a British operation, went into high gear at this point) and their fellow travelers. As always with Jay, cause and effect are reversed, as if the actions of firefighters were to be blamed for the depredations of arsonists. The Israeli "incursion" into Jenin, for example, is treated by people like Jay as if it had nothing whatever to do with the series of suicide bombings, culminating with the Passover massacre that immediately preceded it.

Jenin was reoccupied in April 2002 after the suicide bombing at the Park Hotel in Netanya on Passover evening, March 27. Jenin was the base of the terrorist infrastructure: most of the bombers were "educated" in Jenin, worked in Jenin, trained in Jenin, or passed through Jenin to be "blessed" before going out to kill Jews. Of some one hundred terrorists who carried out suicide bombings between October 2000 and April 2002, twenty-three were sent directly from Jenin. Prior to the Passover slaughter, the supposedly tough Sharon had done little more in response to the almost daily murder of Israeli citizens than make blustery speeches and then turn the other cheek, or bulldoze or bomb empty buildings belonging to the Palestinian Authority. He had seemed far more inclined to the Christian precept "Resist not evil" than were the Christian ministers of Europe who were excoriating him for that "bulldozer mentality." (It does not require a powerful imagination to guess how France or Germany or America would deal with a "Jenin" that dispatched murderers to butcher French or German or American citizens on a daily basis. Of one thing we can be sure: there would have been no bulldozers for Mr. Jay to complain of and also no twenty-three dead Israeli soldiers in Jenin, because the terrorist headquarters would have been obliterated by aerial bombing—and there really might have been not fifty dead Palestinians [most of them fighters] in Jenin but the "genocide of thousands," the "Jeningrad" trumpeted by Jay's favorite news media.)

Thirty Jews were killed and 140 injured at the Netanya seder table, a desecration of a holy place as flagrant as any in recent memory. But Jay's compassion is reserved for the victims of *real* "atrocities," such as "the cruel and vindictive destruction of the venerable olive groves under the pretext that they were hiding places for snipers" (24). Pretext? On October 30, 2002, Israel Radio reported that the terrorist who murdered two girls, ages one and fourteen, and also a woman in Hermesh exploited the olive trees that reach up to the community located between Mevo Dotan and Baka al-Gharbiya, some six kilometers west of the Green Line in northern Samaria. The trees had indeed provided cover that made it possible for the killer first to reconnoiter the area in advance—as an olive harvester—and then to slip under the fence to do his murderous work.

Jay's congenital inability to report anything accurately is also apparent in his allusion to Adam Shapiro, offered as an instance of the atrocities visited by *American* Jews on people whose only sin is "criticism of Israeli policies" (22). He identifies Shapiro as "the idealistic . . . American Jewish peace activist" (22). Whatever Shapiro is, he is not a peace activist; he is a Yasser Arafat activist. A leader of the International Solidarity Movement founded by his wife, Huwaida Arraf, his "idealism" consisted of offering himself as a human shield (also breakfast companion) for Arafat in Ramallah, in the hope of making it easier for the archterrorist to murder Jewish children with impunity. His "criticism of Israeli policies" consisted of celebrating "suicide operations" as "noble" and urging that violence is a necessity of "Palestinian resistance."

One might expect that Jay would do better in reporting on Jewish misdeeds that "cause" the release of untidy emotions in antisemites when these misdeeds occur right under his nose, so to speak. But in fact the most egregious example of deceptive reporting in his essay is his account of an event on his own (Berkeley) campus. It reads as follows: "When literally thousands of emails and withdrawals of substantial alumni donations to the University of California at Berkeley followed the disclosure that a course description for an English class . . . endorsed the Palestinian position, it becomes abundantly clear how concerted the effort has become to punish dissenters from Sharon's heavy-handed policies" (22–23). And here is the description (not provided by Jay, needless to add) of that course, offered by one Snehal Shingavi:

> The Politics and Poetics of Palestinian Resistance:
>
> Since the inception of the intifada in September 2000, Palestinians have been fighting for their right to exist. The brutal Israeli military occupation of Palestine, an occupation that has been ongoing since 1948, has systematically displaced, killed, and maimed millions of Palestinian people. And yet, from under the brutal weight of the occupation, Palestinians have produced their own culture and poetry of resistance. This class will examine the history of the Palestinian resistance . . . in order to produce an understanding of the Intifada and to develop a coherent political analysis of the situation. This class takes as its starting point the right of Palestinians to fight for their own self-determination. Conservative thinkers are encouraged to seek other sections.

For Jay, this polemical balderdash—reeking of Stalinist pedagogy, a violation of the very idea of a university, and a blatant call for violence against Israelis and destruction of their state, supported by a booklist that covers the whole gamut of political opinion about Palestinian "resistance," from the omnipresent Edward Said (three separate titles) to Norman Finkelstein (discussed earlier in this book)—is nothing more than "dissent" from the policies of Sharon (who is not even mentioned in the description). The real culprit in Jay's eyes is not the puffed-up insurrectionary who conceived this obscene travesty of "an English class," but the people who have the temerity to criticize it. And somehow he knows that, in a state where millions of people consider themselves to be "conservative thinkers," all the objectors were Jews.[14]

Coming to the defense of Jews and Israel has never attracted timorous people; and to do so in a place like Berkeley, where mob rule prevented Benjamin Netanyahu (in September 2000) from giving a lecture in the city, and where cadres of Arab and leftist students can shut down campus buildings and disrupt final exams whenever the anti-Israel fit is upon them, may even require a special degree of courage. Jews who assign responsibility for anti-Jewish aggression to Jewish misbehavior not only save themselves from the unpleasant and often dangerous task of coming to the defense of the Jews under attack, but also retain the delightful charms of good conscience. Hitler's professors (to borrow the title of Max Weinreich's famous book of 1946[15]) were the first to make antisemitism both academically respectable and complicit in murder. They have now been succeeded by Arafat's professors: not only the boycotters, not only the advocates of suicide bombings, but also the fellow travelers like Martin Jay.

Notes

1. Quoted in David Horowitz, *Radical Son* (New York: Simon & Schuster, 1997), 176.
2. The full text of Summers's speech may be found in *Congress Monthly* (September/October 2003).
3. "No, It Isn't Anti-Semitic," *London Review of Books*, August 21, 2003.
4. Hannah Arendt, *The Origins of Totalitarianism*, 3 vols. (New York: Harcourt, Brace & World, 1951), 3: 138.
5. See Edward Alexander, "The Academic Boycott of Israel: Back to 1933?" *Jerusalem Post*, January 3, 2003; "Evil Educators Defend the Indefensible," *Jerusalem Post*, January 10, 2003; and "Suicide Bombing 101," *American Spectator*, June/July 2001, 28–30.
6. David Caute, *The Fellow-Travellers: Intellectual Friends of Communism* (New Haven, CT: Yale University Press, 1988).
7. Martin Peretz, "Traveling with Bad Companions," *Los Angeles Times*, June 23, 2003.
8. Subsequent page references to Martin Jay's essay will be in parentheses in the text.
9. Albert Lindemann, *Esau's Tears: Modern Anti-Semitism and the Rise of the Jews* (Cambridge: Cambridge University Press, 1997), 308, 311, 291, 140–41, 496, 54.
10. Paul Breines, *Tough Jews: Political Fantasies and the Moral Dilemma of American Jewry* (New York: Basic Books, 1990).
11. Ruth R. Wisse, *If I Am Not for Myself . . . The Liberal Betrayal of the Jews* (New York: Free Press, 1992), 138.
12. Arendt, *Origins of Totalitarianism*, 3:138.

13.   Quoted in Rosie DiManno, "Unlike Victims, Bomber Died without Pain,"
      Toronto Star, June 19, 2002.
14.   In a well-hidden place, n. 33, Jay acknowledges that "some of the outcry"
      about the course had to do with its last sentence telling conservative think-
      ers to get lost, but he is confident that "the main reason for the response
      was the content of the course" (p. 28). Another Berkeley faculty member,
      who teaches in the English department, provided me with the following
      description of the incident, which may be instructive:

> I don't think that any chairman would dare disallow such a class on politi-
> cal grounds for fear of PC [Political Correctness] extortion. Of course, the
> crucial point—that such a class has nothing to do with English—doesn't
> even enter the picture since so many English composition classes have
> been politicized . . . that it's hard to imagine an English chair eager to
> defend the teaching of grammar and logic. Hence, the brazenness of the
> instructor who wrote that course description: without the statement that
> conservatives were not welcome (which is discriminatory), the pedagogy
> and politics of the course would have been unassailable in the current
> climate. One thing I distinctly remember with regard to the Palestinian
> composition class incident was that it coincided with a very loud anti-
> Israel rally—louder than the anti-war demonstration last week.

15.   Max Weinreich, *Hitler's Professors: The Part of Scholarship in Hitler's Crimes
      against the Jewish People* (New York: YIVO, 1946).

10

Michael Lerner: Hillary Clinton's Jewish Rasputin (1995, 2014)

In May 1993 a flurry of newspaper and magazine articles revealed that Hillary Clinton's crusade to bring the reign of virtue to a selfish and benighted America was to be carried out under the spiritual tutelage of Michael Lerner, the Jewish leftist "thinker," self-promoter, and editor of *Tikkun* magazine, a publication itself dedicated (according to its official motto appearing in each issue) "to heal, repair and transform the world." Lerner, it turned out, had visited the White House to instruct the first lady in "the politics of meaning" and also of "caring and sharing." "As Michael Lerner and I discussed," Mrs. Clinton announced, "we have to first create a language that would better communicate what we are trying to say, and the policies would flow from that language."[1]

To people not beguiled by Lerner, his "language" is redolent less of mind than of pudding and corn mush. "I proposed that the Clinton Administration establish a policy where, for any proposed legislation... there would have to be written first an Ethical and Community Environmental Impact Report... to report how the proposed legislation or new program would impact on shaping the ethics and the caring and sharing of the community covered by that agency." "The 1970s and '80s in the U.S. were dominated," Lerner has written, "by this belief that the individual had only him/herself [rather than 'the system'] to blame if s/he faced a life that was unfulfilling."[2] (Although a very slovenly writer, Lerner is a diligent gender warden and pronoun policeman.) Insofar as readers could penetrate the New Age pseudo-jargon that emanated from this odd couple, it appeared that Lerner had promised to distill for Mrs. Clinton the essence of the ethical ideas of the Bible for application to public policy. She had, moreover, proved a ready pupil, one who could say to him, with characteristic elegance, at a White House reception, "Am I your mouthpiece or what?"[3]

Who, everybody began to ask, was the first lady's new "guru"? Journalists with poor memories or a weak instinct for research mistakenly referred to him as being—prior to his elevation by the Clintons—"welcomed virtually nowhere."[4] In fact, however, he had been a favorite of the news media ever since he began, in 1986, to promote the "Palestinian" cause within the Jewish community, where his name has been a familiar one since the late 1960s, partly for his aggression against that community itself, partly because of his involvement in radical causes generally.

In fall 1969 Lerner commenced his open battle with what he likes to call "the Jewish establishment" of "fat cats and conformists" in an article entitled "Jewish New Leftism at Berkeley" in *Judaism* magazine. It included such utterances as the following: "The Jewish community is racist, internally corrupt, and an apologist for the worst aspects of American capitalism and imperialism." "Black anti-Semitism is a tremendous disgrace to Jews; for this is not an anti-Semitism rooted in . . . hatred of the Christ-killers but rather one rooted in the concrete fact of oppression by Jews of blacks in the ghetto . . . in part an earned anti-Semitism." ". . . The synagogue as currently established will have to be smashed." "This anti-Zionism [of young Jews] is irrational in its conclusions [that Israel should be destroyed]" but "I know it to be correct in its fundamental impulses."[5] The publication of his article, which expressed views difficult to distinguish from those of non-Jewish anti-semites, led to the resignation of some of the editors of the magazine (one of whom moved to *Commentary*).

A few months later, in a February 22, 1970, interview in the *Seattle Times*, Lerner predicted that he would be fired from his academic post (as visiting assistant professor) at the University of Washington because "I dig Marx," and that "three years from now I don't expect to be alive. I'm too public a person." At least one of these predictions came true when, on March 3, the philosophy department voted against renewing Lerner's appointment. Although many students alleged that Lerner used his classes to recruit members for his Seattle Liberation Front (which, he used to boast, was the nation's largest, most active white radical group),[6] and State Senator James Andersen (later a state supreme court justice) said the taxpayers were "fed up to their ears with paying Lerner to teach violence," the philosophy faculty insisted that Lerner was being denied reappointment solely because his qualifications did not measure up to those of other applicants for the two positions open. Lerner, however, disputed the very right of the faculty to make decisions about a Marxist like himself: "It is ludicrous for any member of this department to judge me, just as I wouldn't be qualified to judge a logician." Like his own Seattle Liberation Front, which presented the "non-negotiable" demand that a mass meeting of "the people" be summoned to vote on his reappointment, Lerner accused the faculty of usurping power: "That power has to be taken from them."[7] But neither these threats nor the Bacchanalian protests of Lerner's followers during the philosophers' deliberations (according to the *Seattle Times*, one Lerner supporter, "a small girl in jeans, bare from the waist up, ran back and forth along the table twice while the meeting went on") could save the day.[8]

Lerner promptly announced that "I can't get a job anywhere because of my political views. . . . My own case is further proof that working for change in America through the normal channels . . . is a useless strategy. The only place left for those who want social change is to be fighting in the streets."[9] Two days later Lerner helped to organize a series of demonstrations at the university that culminated on March 11 when his followers in the Seattle Liberation Front (SLF) joined with the Black Student Union to form a combined mob of 1,500–2,000 that invaded six university buildings and brutally beat at least fourteen instructors and students who did not heed their "strike" order. (Lerner, if we can judge from newspaper photos, remained at a safe distance, bullhorn in hand.) The issue in question, lest one forget to mention it, was indeed a momentous one: the refusal of the university to cancel an athletic competition with the Mormon Brigham Young University, which Lerner had labeled a racist institution because it did not admit blacks to its priesthood. Lerner's SLF declared that "the issue of racism . . . cannot be debated, but must be eliminated."[10] Impatience with debate had already been in evidence in early February, when Steve Weiner, editor of the *University of Washington Daily*, was roughed up for an editorial that campus radicals deemed "racist."

In spring 1970 (June 2), Lerner sued Slade Gorton, then attorney general of Washington state (later U.S. senator) for libel, claiming two million dollars in damages. Gorton, in a May 13 speech in Walla Walla, had described Lerner's SLF as "totally indistinguishable from fascism and Nazism." Lerner contended that this remark prejudiced his right to a fair trial on a conspiracy indictment stemming from a February 17,

1970, demonstration in which members of the SLF had broken store windows and lobbed tear gas and paint bombs at the U.S. courthouse in downtown Seattle. In reply to Lerner's libel suit, Gorton said that "I would suggest to Professor Lerner that if he can't stand the heat of public discussion he may withdraw from the scene." At the end of June, when state attorneys were about to ask for a dismissal of Lerner's suit on grounds that it was "an infringement of free speech," Lerner (sometime leader of Berkeley's Free Speech Movement) withdrew the suit.[11]

Lerner's sayings and doings of decades ago would not merit more attention than we usually give to the origins of an ambitious public figure's politics—unless they served to reveal a startling continuity between the Lerner who in 1969 advocated the "smashing" of synagogues and the Lerner who relentlessly advocates the Palestinian "liberation movement," no mean hand at synagogue-smashing itself. "Our deeds still travel with us from afar," wrote George Eliot in *Middlemarch*, "and what we have been makes us what we are."

In his *Judaism* essay of 1969, Lerner had singled out the journal *Commentary* for special scorn as the instrument of the Jewish "establishment" in league with "the American ruling class," "American imperialism," and "racism" (because it had criticized black antisemitism). In 1986 he gained greater prominence by founding *Tikkun* as a kind of antimagazine, which took its primary meaning and purpose from the desire to pull down *Commentary* (and its secondary one, as noted above, from the modest aim "to heal, repair and transform the world"). In its first issue Anne Roiphe sounded the favorite theme of the youthful Lerner by damning contributors to *Commentary* as "Court Jews of the Right" (an epithet that may have returned to haunt Lerner as he stalked the corridors of the White House). At Jewish conferences young *Tikkun* hucksters peddled anti-*Commentary* t-shirts.

The zeal with which *Tikkun* argued the Palestinian cause within the Jewish community soon made Lerner a favorite display Jew of the news media: a yarmulke-wearing, rotund beard-plucker[12] of vaguely "rabbinic" appearance who could always be relied on to blame Israel and not the Arabs for the absence of peace, and to liken Israeli defense against Palestinian Arab violence to "medieval Christian mobs . . . organizing pogroms against the whole Jewish community."[13] His denunciatory comments on the intifada seemed "perfectly right" to Professor Edward Said, member of the Palestine National Council, adviser to Arafat, and ideologue of terror. (Said was a major speaker at *Tikkun*'s December 1988 conference in New York.) Since Lerner fitted perfectly into the popular journalistic conception of "prophetic" Judaism as reaching its apotheosis in St. Marx and the left wing of the Democratic party,[14] he was crowned by the ever-predictable *New York Times* and the major television networks as philosopher king of American Jewry, the ultimate authority on the manifold misdeeds of Israel.

Once the *intifada* got under way, it was hard to watch American television or read the American press for very long without becoming aware that Michael Lerner himself had become, if not quite the Jewish establishment, then the omnipresent, gentile-appointed voice of the Jewish community. Yet his antiestablishment rhetoric remained very much what it had been in 1969–70. Thus, on February 24, 1989, the *New York Times* afforded him space to hold forth, in a typically self-serving piece, on the way in which the voice of progressive Jews like himself, "the silenced majority" who were "appalled by Israel's brutal repression of the Palestinian uprising," had been "stifled" by the "establishment leadership." Never before had a stifled voice been heard by so many millions, or been trumpeted with such metronomic regularity. In fact, Lerner's *Times* essay was soon reprinted, with some variations, in the March 17 issue of the *Jerusalem Post*.

Now, even more absurdly than in 1969, Lerner pictured himself as both the true voice of the people and a lonely knight, a sensitive soul sallying forth to confront a mob of thick-skinned conformist louts who would eat him alive if they could. Meanwhile, this self-proclaimed dissenter consented to the prejudices of at least half the world in blaming Israel for the state of war forced upon it by the Arabs and for defending itself against the organized violence of the intifada. (For good measure, he characteristically suggested [*American Journal of Sociology*, November 1988] that Israel's existence and the tendency of Diaspora Jews to identify with the Jewish state were creating anti-semitism in the third world.) After organizing ads in the spring of 1988 calling for Israel to "end the occupation"—typical products of those American Jews who would like to rule Israel from northern California or Manhattan—Lerner told the press that for such an enterprise "courage is necessary," and that he had received death threats in the mail.[15] (Presumably they were being filed alongside the ones he intimated receiving in 1970.) Not content to aid the Palestinian cause in the temporal realm alone, Lerner, in the fall, instructed the *Tikkun* faithful to devote Yom Kippur to contrition for Jewish mistreatment of the Palestinian Arabs—prompting long-time Labor Zionist Marie Syrkin to observe, in December 1988 (two months before her death), that "the 'progressive' Jewish magazine, *Tikkun*, recently exhorted the Jewish people to observe the Day of Atonement (remember Yom Kippur, 1973?) with an orgy of confession of 'collective guilt.' What sanctimonious chutzpah if not accompanied by the breast-beatings of far greater sinners!"[16] In April 1989, when Prime Minister Shamir visited Washington, Lerner organized an ad in the *New York Times*, diligently rounding up the Jewish petition-signers always ready to spill their ink on behalf of those who spill Jewish blood. The ad, designed to undercut Israel's bargaining position, not only ordered Shamir to negotiate with the PLO, but (with Lerner's customary modesty) told him that negotiations must culminate in a PLO state.

The invasion of Kuwait by Iraq in 1990 seems to have caught Lerner, like the Kuwaitis, off guard. The standard anti-Israel line was "linkage," as set forth by, for example, *Tikkun* contributing editor Milton Viorst, who told the magazine's readers (January/February 1991) that "the disappearance of Kuwait would not be one of the great tragedies of history," but also that the root cause of the Gulf War as of all other Middle Eastern problems was the "atmosphere of instability" created by the ultimate villain of the region: Israel. Lerner too advocated linkage between Iraq's invasion of Kuwait and Israel's "occupation" of the disputed territories, but with a difference. In September (see *Washington Jewish Week*, September 20), "after deep soul-searching," he opposed reliance on economic sanctions against the Iraqi invaders and exhorted the U.S. "to quickly escalate the struggle against Iraq." But he added that, in order to conciliate "moderate Arab allies," American military intervention should be "linked" to a promise "to put massive pressure on Israel to agree to a Palestinian state." In other words, the Arabs should receive huge bribes, paid in Israeli currency, for doing America the great favor of allowing it to defend their interests.

By January, however, Lerner—terrified to find himself dissenting from the conformity of dissent against impending war—realigned himself with the orthodox definition of linkage, opposed the war, urged reliance on economic sanctions, blamed Bush for not acceding to Saddam Hussein's demand for an international conference, and claimed that his position on the Gulf crisis had all along been as constant as the Northern Star.

About two months after the Scud missiles had stopped raining down on Israel, Michael Lerner betook himself and the *Tikkun* entourage to Israel to preside over a June conference entitled "How to End the Occupation: A Strategy for the Peace Movement." The conference manifesto displayed the openness to debate that Lerner had learned in Berkeley's

Free Speech Movement and practiced at the University of Washington: "To create a safe space for this discussion, we invite you only if you already agree that Israel should enter negotiations aimed at creating a demilitarized Palestinian state."[17] The conference's overriding purpose was to recommend ways to disturb what Lerner disparaged as the "quiet daily life" of Israelis, "protected from having to confront the moral outrage of . . . Israeli oppression of Palestinians." Lerner, surveying Israeli life from the distant perch of his ethical superiority, had concluded that the Israelis were too much at ease in Zion. Apparently dissatisfied with the little disturbances visited upon Israelis by Iraqi missiles; bombs exploding in nurseries, school, and supermarkets; or stabbings and shootings carried out in the buses and streets, he recommended "bringing the war home" by "disrupting the daily operation of Israeli society" (*Jerusalem Post*, July 13, 1991). One of the best ways of doing this would be for Israelis to refuse to do military service if assigned to serve in the disputed territories. Before the Israeli authorities could decide whether Lerner, a foreigner, should be prosecuted for incitement and sedition, he was back in the United States, struggling with the unquiet daily life of a prophet (and also claiming [*LA Times*, July 30, 1991] that his remarks, intended only for "internal discussion," had been taken out of context). Although the conference brochure announced that "WE WILL BE ASKING THE TOUGH QUESTIONS," Lerner and his acolytes seem to have overlooked the distinctly ethical (if not very tough) question of how an American Jew is justified in advocating, and even working to force upon Israel, concessions to Palestinian Arabs that bring risks that will be borne by Israeli Jews alone.

Not long after returning from Israel, Lerner found himself faced with intricate foreign policy decisions. Soon he would have to decide whether he could "dissent" from American policy as readily as he had just done from Israeli policy. The American administration, having failed to achieve the primary war aim of removing Hussein from power, decided to pursue, yet again, the idea of a regional peace conference. As always, George H. W. Bush and James Baker could discern but a single "obstacle to peace" in the region: Jewish settlements in Judea and Samaria. Therefore, in summer 1991, Bush decided to force Israel, in advance of any negotiations, to freeze settlements by reneging on his longstanding promise to recommend U.S. guarantees of a ten-billion-dollar bank loan for meeting the housing and employment needs of a huge immigration from the USSR. In his press conference of September 12, 1991, Bush depicted American Jews as an alien presence in the American body politic, a conglomeration of "powerful political forces," "a thousand lobbyists" besieging poor, helpless Bush, "one lonely little guy down here." The president did not hesitate to use the basest slanders of the anti-Israel propagandist's trade. This veteran backroom politician painted American Jewish "lobbyists" as a fifth column in their own country, contriving schemes to steal the Wheaties from American breakfast tables so that Israeli Jews could periodically be showered with thousand-dollar bills. He suggested (in a rewriting of history worthy of the Stalinists) that American lives had been risked in the Gulf War in order to defend Israel.

The professional "Jewish critics of Israel" had, of course, preceded Bush in urging that aid for absorption of immigrants be made contingent on Israel's cessation of settlement activity in the territories. In the *New York Times* of July 16, 1991, for example, David Biale, Lerner's loyal bulldog, recommended that America withhold aid to immigrants in order to pressure Israel to accept Arab terms for a peace settlement. If Bush's statements of September 12 had merely done precisely what Lerner and the other Jewish apostates from the Jewish community had for years been urging presidents to do, their approval of his performance would hardly merit notice. But Bush had done something more than use the immigrants as hostages to force Israel to surrender Judea and Samaria prior to peace talks: he had also demonstrated a keen awareness of, and a still keener desire to exploit, the fact that antisemitism is a light sleeper.

Yet Lerner not only was unperturbed by Bush's cynical exploitation of anti-Jewish resentment; he applauded it. Back in June he had excoriated Bush for suspending the U.S. "dialogue" with the PLO merely because Arafat had been escalating his terror campaign against Jews. But now (*New York Times*, September 16) Lerner declared his great satisfaction with Bush's action and said that the loss of the loan guarantee, the arousal of antisemitism, and the breakdown of American-Israeli relations were "the fault of Shamir, not Bush." It was, according to Lerner, tough lobbying in Washington by American Jews that threatened to stir up antisemitism. Israel, moreover, was guilty of the sin of trying "to use the Russian Jews to solve the demographic gap." At that moment it must have occurred to Lerner that, at least to unprogressive Jewish minds, serving as a haven for Jews in flight from persecution and striving for a Jewish majority in the land of Israel come very close to defining the nature of Zionism and the purpose of the Jewish state. He therefore hastened to assure his interviewer that he was really

"very pro-Israel," a tactic that in later years would be employed by such
Jewish anti-Israel organizations as Jewish Voice for Peace and J Street.
Despite this claim, he earned high marks from Patrick Buchanan two
days later in a column that excoriated Israel and Jewry in general, but
made exception for two deserving Jews: the virulent antisemite Israel
Shahak, and Michael Lerner. Lerner's lifelong tendency to play the
(fraudulent) role of "dissenter" from the Jewish community (a community that wields no power over, and therefore poses no threat to,
dissenters) had now made him a bedfellow of the Republicans. In March
1992 he was still lauding Bush for "a form of tough love that is actually
in the best interests of the Jewish people," and insisting that "he [Bush]
needs to be congratulated and supported."[18] It is not known whether
the Clintons were paying close attention to Lerner's statements at this
early stage of the presidential campaign.

Although it might at first seem that the man nearly anointed the Jewish Rasputin to Hillary Clinton bears little resemblance to the ferocious
radical who in 1970 wielded a bullhorn and posed for photographs in
front of the hammer and sickle, in fact Lerner merits congratulation for
the extraordinary consistency of his first principles (or primal instincts)
in the more than four decades of his public career. He was speaking
the truth when in an interview of November 1989 (*East Bay Express*)
he said, "I've been on the same path all along. I haven't shifted since I
was twelve years old as far as I can see."

The mainspring of his career has been the abandonment of his own
people when they are under attack, whether by antisemitic blacks or
by PLO killers (and their countless apologists) or by unscrupulous
and powerful politicians like the first President Bush, or by his two
favorite recent mentors, John J. Mearsheimer and Stephen M. Walt.
He admires and promotes their "careful and thoughtful work" about
"the Israel Lobby," which falls short only because they lack his inside
knowledge of the Jewish world. Therefore they neglect to point out, as
only a latter-day Nicholas Donin can, that the Jewish conspiracy extends
well beyond government to "the vast number of Jewish institutions and
even . . . synagogues, and families that impose on their members a
certain discipline that goes well beyond any normal political party or
force." This, Cynthia Ozick has observed, is the language of the *Protocols
of the Elders of Zion*.[19]

Lerner's abandonment has always come dressed in the long robes of
the prophets of "ethical idealism." Now, as in 1969, Lerner blames the
Jews—this time mainly the Israeli Jews—for the murderous hostility,

the "earned anti-Semitism," of their "oppressed" enemies. His methods too remain, in essentials, unchanged. In 1970, as we have noted, he tried to quash criticism of the thuggish tactics of his Seattle Liberation Front by litigation. In spring 1989 I submitted an essay about Lerner to several Jewish papers, including the *Jerusalem Post*. The *Post* and *Washington Jewish Week* accepted the piece yet never published it. An explanation for its mysterious fate was offered by Susan Rosenbluth, editor of the (New Jersey) *Jewish Voice*, who reported in her June 1989 issue that, in an interview with her, "Mr. Lerner said he intends to sue publications that print Dr. Alexander's piece."

"The child is father of the man," wrote Wordsworth. The twenty-seven-year-old Michael Lerner, who in 1970 sported a bandana, is the father of the man who twenty-five years later would play with his rabbinical skullcap before a background of Jewish books for the TV cameras. Still sick with self-love, still dramatizing his courage as a "public person," still blaming the Jews for the aggression of their enemies, Lerner has grown fat on the intifadas and used the constant burden of peril of the people of Israel as an opportunity for self-aggrandizement. For these efforts he was rewarded by being elevated, to borrow a phrase from *Tikkun* magazine, to the status of Court Jew of the Left. Or was the first lady really enraptured by his vapid maunderings about the politics of meaning? Let us hope that the sentimentally Christian Mrs. Clinton, whose theology tends to be formed by her politics, sees in Lerner only an exotic purveyor of Jewish-accented leftism and not a Jewish exponent of "liberation theology" who has given to it the original twist of wishing to discredit rather than liberate the community from which he comes and the homeland to which it is attached.

So far there is no evidence that Lerner poured his ideas on the world's need for an irredentist Palestinian state into Mrs. Clinton's ear during their White House meeting of April 26, 1993. But now that she is seriously thinking of making another run for the White House—as president, not merely first lady—and now that Lerner has become a rabbi of sorts and head of something called The Network of Spiritual Progressives (for whom support of the Palestinian cause is the litmus test of progressivism), we should not be surprised if he makes a second run at the role of Rasputin. Besides, he does recall having told her, "Gee, I have so many things that we ought to discuss," and she replied, "Well, we don't have to do it all today; this is just the first of several meetings."[20]

Notes

1. Michael Kelly, "Saint Hillary," *New York Times Magazine*, May 23, 1993, 63.
2. Edward Rothstein, "Broken Vessel," *New Republic*, March 6, 1989, 19.
3. Henry Allen, "A New Phrase at the White House," *Washington Post*, June 9, 1993.
4. Thomas Fields-Meyer, "This Year's Prophet," *New York Times Magazine*, June 27, 1993, 28.
5. Michael P. Lerner, "Jewish New Leftism at Berkeley," *Judaism* 18 (Fall 1969): 474–76.
6. *New York Times*, April 26, 1970.
7. *Seattle Times*, March 4, 1970. After his arrival at the White House, Lerner told Anne Gowen of the *Washington Times* (June 7, 1993) that "I am not now, nor ever have been, a Marxist."
8. In 1991 Lerner sent a barrage of letters to university administrators, Seattle city officials, and Seattle newspaper editors urging the University of Washington to repent for its transgression of 1970 by rehiring him (*Seattle Times*, February 6, 1991).
9. *Seattle Times*, March 4, 1970.
10. *Seattle Times*, March 6, 1970; *University of Washington Daily*, March 9, 1970.
11. *Seattle Post-Intelligencer*, February 18, June 3, and June 30, 1970. Lerner and seven others were charged with conspiring to damage federal property. They were tried in Tacoma in November 1970. Deciding to put the court on trial, Lerner and the others disrupted proceedings and draped a swastika over Judge George Boldt's bench, shouting, "Heil Hitler!" They refused to return to court when ordered, causing a mistrial to be declared—followed by a riot between some defendants and marshals. Lerner spent ten weeks at California's Terminal Island federal penitentiary for contempt of court. The original charges were never refiled.
12. Not long after an earlier version of this article appeared in 1988, Lerner shaved his beard.
13. *Moment*, June 1990, 33.
14. Irving Howe caused consternation at one *Tikkun* conference (December 1988) by stating the obvious: there is no sanction in Jewish religion for liberal politics. "To claim there is a connection," said Howe, "can lead to parochial sentimentalism or ethnic vanity." See Rothstein, "Broken Vessel," 19.
15. *Jerusalem Post*, 26 April 1988.
16. *Midstream*, 34 (December 1988): 31.
17. See Ze'ev Chafetz, "Why I'm Not Going to *Tikkun* Conference in Israel," *Northern California Jewish Bulletin*, 21 June 1991.
18. *New York Times*, 19 March 1992.
19. "Apostasy, Then and Now," in *Israel's Jewish Defamers* (Boston: CAMERA, 2008).
20. *Washington Times*, 7 June 1993.

11

Ashamed Jews:
The Finkler Question
(2010)

"When a man can no longer be a Jew, he becomes a Zionist."
—A character named Yudka in "The Sermon,"
by Haim Hazaz (1942)

"I am a Jew by virtue of the fact that I am not a Zionist."
—A character named Kugle in *The Finkler Question*,
by Howard Jacobson (2010)

The Finkler Question is a profoundly serious comic novel. Seriousness, let us remember, is not the same as solemnity; it does not require pince-nez spectacles and grave demeanor. Howard Jacobson's primary subject is the English version of Jewish hatred of Israel, otherwise known as the antisemitism of Jews in its most recent incarnation. It is a serious subject because Jewish Israel-haters and Jewish "anorexics" (who wish the Jews to live without a body) play an enormously disproportionate role in the blackening of Israel's image and the relentless tightening of the international noose around its throat. If they have not set it in motion, they have certainly accelerated a process that may turn out to be the antecedent of a second Holocaust within a single century. Such Jews have already made a large contribution to antisemitic agit-prop and the raw violence consequent upon it in England. Jacobson presents both with a specificity, courage, and candor rare among Jewish novelists, although they had already been the subject of several books by English writers, most notably *The Resurgence of Antisemitism* (2006) by the philosopher and literary critic Bernard Harrison, and *Trials of the Diaspora* (2010) by literary critic and historian Anthony Julius.

At the novel's center stands a womanizing gentile named Julian Treslove, formerly a programmer for the BBC (the butt of relentless and well-deserved derision throughout the novel) and then a double for various celebrities. When at school he had befriended a Jew (the first he had ever known) named Samuel Finkler; both were students of the transplanted Czech Jew Libor Sevcik, who later became a celebrity journalist. Treslove came to think of Finkler as representing (although in ways he finds difficult to define) Jews in general, and it is this mis-apprehension that explains the novel's title: a "Finkler" is for Treslove "a Jew," and *The Finkler Question* really means *The Jewish Question.* Partly because his own life has been a series of romantic misadventures, partly because he convinces himself that he's been mugged by a woman who thinks he's a Jew, and partly because he aspires to substitute the Jewish tragedy for his private farce, Julian aspires to (yet never does) become a Jew. The novel is full of his (often jejune) questions about what it means "to think Jewishly," to speak Jewishly, to eat Jewishly. But he also is puzzled—and one really should sympathize with him and with all the gentiles he represents for their understandable befuddlement—by the fact that so many of the Jew-haters he has known are Jews: "I remember what anti-Semites they all were there [at the BBC], especially the Jews."[1]

Finkler, who studied moral philosophy at Oxford and has named two of his children after Kant (Immanuel) and Pascal (Blaise), has become rich and famous by publishing a series of self-help books of moral philosophy. Among the more delicious titles are: *The Existentialist in the Kitchen, The Little Book of Household Stoicism*, and *The Socratic Flirt: How to Reason Your Way into a Better Sex Life.* (The titles call to mind the writings of Alain De Botton, another "proud" Anglo-Jewish atheist and author of such "practical" manuals as *How Proust Can Change Your Life.*) We enter the story shortly after Finkler has vaulted to still greater fame by concluding his appearance on the popular BBC program *Desert Island Discs* with the declaration that, "as a Jew," he was "ashamed," that is to say, ashamed of Israel (a word that he did not, however, allow to soil his lips, sticking to "Palestine," or even "Canaan"). For this gesture he is promptly rewarded with an invitation to join a group of "well-known theatrical and academic Jews" who offer to rename themselves "in honour of his courage in speaking out—Ashamed Jews." Flattered by the attention of (mostly third-rate) actors—for the professors' praise he cares as little as for "the prayers he had never said for his grandfather" (113–15)—he accepts, on the condition (quickly agreed to) that they slightly change their name to

ASHamed Jews to show off their contempt for Holocaust memory: "Holocaust fucking Holocaust" (291). (Jacobson's unfortunate addiction to this epithet is on the gargantuan scale of Hollywood directors and other linguistically deprived and morally anemic types who believe people actually talk like this.)

"ASHamed Jews" is a wonderful comic invention, on a par with Philip Roth's Antisemites Anonymous in *Operation Shylock*. It produces (and is produced by) Jacobson's best writing:

> The logic that made it impossible for those who had never been Zionists to call themselves ASHamed Zionists did not extend to Jews who had never been Jews. To be an ASHamed Jew did not require that you had been knowingly Jewish all your life. Indeed, one among them only found out he was Jewish at all in the course of making a television programme in which he was confronted on camera with *who he really was*. In the final frame of the film he was disclosed weeping before a memorial in Auschwitz to dead ancestors who until that moment he had never known he'd had. 'It could explain where I get my comic genius from,' he told an interviewer for a newspaper, though by then he had renegotiated his new allegiance. Born a Jew on Monday, he had signed up to be an ASHamed Jew by Wednesday and was seen chanting 'We are all Hezbollah' outside the Israeli Embassy on the following Saturday. (138–39)

Readers unfamiliar with the current English scene may assume that Jacobson's comic triumph derives from his exaggeration of "reality." Is there actually a liberal rabbi in St. John's Wood who always wears a PLO scarf when riding his motorbike to shul every morning? Can there be a real-life model for Alvin Poliakov, who presides over an anticircumcision website called "ifnotnowwhen.com" that recounts his valiant struggle to reverse his circumcision and—for no extra charge—tells his readers how "sexual mutilation . . . is just one more of the countless offences against humanity [along with Zionism] to be laid at the gates of the Jews" (201).

In fact, Jacobson exaggerates nothing; quite the contrary. The reality of Anglo-Jewish dementia about Israel outruns even the daring of Jacobson's imagination. What novelist would dare to imagine the famous Anglo-Jewish historian Eric Hobsbawm (fellow of the British Academy, Companion of Honour, fellow of the Royal Society of Literature) holding forth as follows to his neighbor in Wales, David Pryce-Jones? "At a dinner to which we were both invited, he first glorified Castro's Cuba to another guest, the British ambassador there at the time, and then went on to say that a nuclear bomb ought to be dropped on Israel, because it was better to kill 5 million Jews now than 200 million innocent people in a world war later. The last person who had reduced genocide to mathematics was Josef Goebbels, I replied, whereupon Hobsbawm got up from the meal and left the house" (*National Review*, October 29, 2012). No such scene appears in Jacobson's novel.

To some extent, *The Finkler Question* is what the French call a *roman à clef*, a novel with a key in which the knowing reader is expected to identify, within the work, actual people or events. Thus most of Jacobson's English readers immediately recognized that Finkler's despicable confession of shame on *Desert Island Discs* exactly duplicated that of Miriam Margolyes, the pudgy little character actress, a few years earlier; and that the tearful comedian who discovered his "Jewishness" while making a TV program was Stephen Fry, a stalwart of Jews for Justice for Palestinians. Among British precursors in the *roman à clef* genre are Thomas Love Peacock's *Nightmare Abbey* (1818) and Aldous Huxley's *Point Counter Point* (1928). But the more important point here is that the ancient task of literature is to begin with the actual world, which is far more fantastic than even the most imaginative writer can contrive, and try to make it more plausible, which is to say more in conformity with what Hannah Arendt, in the *Antisemitism* volume of *The Origins of Totalitarianism*, called "the wheedling voice of common sense." Thus the novel's Holocaust-denying Israeli *yored* drummer is in fact based upon one Gilad Atzmon, who is better known in England for endorsing the ideology of the *Protocols of the Elders of Zion* and describing the burning of British synagogues as a "rational act" in retaliation for Israeli actions. Another of Jacobson's fictional inventions, the play called *Sons of Abraham*, which gets a standing ovation for its equation of "Gaza" with Auschwitz, is not quite as blatant in its deranged espousal of the blood libel as the actual (ten-minutes long) play upon which it is based: Caryl Churchill's highly popular 2009 monstrosity called *Seven Jewish Children—A Play for Gaza*, in which the aforementioned Margolyes appeared. (When, because of this, a Jewish nursing home in Australia withdrew its invitation to her to perform there, she was shocked, simply shocked, that anybody could consider a play showing Jews deliberately killing Arab babies and thirsting for their blood to be antisemitic.)

What is true of these secondary examples of apparent "exaggeration" in the book is still more striking in its primary conceit, the Jews of shame who blush for the existence of a Jewish state. Such displays have been a device of self-aggrandizement by Jewish Israel-haters (and not only in England) for many years. In 2003 the late Tony Judt, one of England's booby-trapped gifts to America, in an almost laughable display of insecurity and self-pity, petulantly complained that "non-Israeli Jews feel themselves once again exposed to criticism and vulnerable to attack for things they didn't do. ... The behavior of a self-described Jewish state affects the way everyone else looks at Jews."[2] In 2005 Jacqueline Rose, who appears in *The Finkler Question* as Tamara Krausz (for whom Zionism is a Coleridgean "demon lover" [230] and she its psychoanalyst), "appalled at what the Israeli nation perpetrated in my name," expressed the wish to live "in a world in which we did not have to be ashamed of shame" and looked forward to curing her shame-sickness by destroying its cause: Israel.[3] When, in the novel, she reaches the point of endorsing the old Christian belief that male Jews menstruate, Finkler's revulsion actually carries him to the other side of a public debate between the ashamed and unashamed Jews. Krausz-Rose is the book's most lurid example of Libor's generalization that "We [Jews] have become a sick people" (193).

These ashamed Jews are in many respects like the assimilated Jews of old, insisting that Jewish particularism, Jewish peoplehood, a Jewish state constitute the sole obstacles to universal brotherhood and peace. But there is a difference. Whereas the motto of the assimilationists, as far back as the 1880s, was "Be a Jew at home and a man in the street," the motto of Jews ashamed of Israel is the opposite: "Be a man at home and a Jew in public." At every opportunity, the Jewish anti-Zionist who can no longer be a Jew at home now introduces his self-righteous and self-loving public display of outrage against Israel with "As a Jew . . ." But here too Jacobson, except for a hint or two, substitutes believable fiction for incredible reality: the introduction now, more often than not, is: "As the Jewish child [or grandchild] of Holocaust victims, I am ashamed of Israel and hope to see it boycotted, punished by sanctions, and removed from the family of nations."

The novel's most incisive and severe critic of Finkler and the Jews of shame in general is Finkler's wife, Tyler—or rather her ghost, because she is already dead when the story begins. Finkler's bereavement binds him to Libor, who is also a widower, despite their (apparent) disagreement over Israel and blushing Jews. A convert (against her husband's wishes, of course) to Judaism, Tyler insists that she is the real Jew in their marriage because she knows the difference between culture and biology, religion and stupid ethnic vanity. She sees Finkler and his anti-Zionist comrades as "profoundly self-important" more than "profoundly ashamed"; she knows why Jews pray every morning that "we may never be put to shame"; for her Finkler and his comrades are "*shande* Jews," which is to say *shame* as in "disgrace . . . they brought shame" (270). It is she who must explain to the puzzled Treslove the grotesque and brazen fakery of anti-Zionists who insist that if Jews don't exist as "a light unto the nations" they don't deserve to exist at all (271).

Although nearly every part of this novel has its comic dimension, the single exception that tests the rule (and also Libor Sevcik) comes more than halfway into the story, and shocks all the more precisely *because* it is an exception. Libor agrees to meet with an old (in both senses of the term) girlfriend of his named Emmy Oppenstein after a hiatus of half a century. As usual with Jacobson, whose sex obsession is on a par with Philip Roth's (and equally wearisome to readers who have long been freed from this mad and cruel master—sex, not Roth), we get a resume of their long-ago affair, with the usual speculation about who undressed whom, and so forth. But then, in the book's greatest dramatic moment, comes this:

> She told him, without tears, without false sentiment, that her twenty-two-year-old grandson had been stabbed in the face and blinded by an Algerian man who had shouted 'God is great' in Arabic, and 'Death to all Jews.'
>
> 'I'm very sorry,' Libor said. 'Did this happen in Algeria?'
>
> 'It happened here, Libor.'
>
> 'In London?'
>
> 'Yes, in London.'
>
> . . . Libor had been lucky in love but in politics he was from a part of the world that expected nothing good of anybody. Jew-hating was back— of course Jew-hating was back. Soon it would be full-blown fascism, Nazis, Stalinism. These things didn't go away. There was nowhere for them to go to. They were indestructible, non-biodegradable. They waited in the great rubbish tip that was the human heart.
>
> It wasn't even the Algerian's fault in the end. He just did what history had told him to do. God is great . . . kill all Jews. It was hard to take offence—unless, of course, the blinded boy was your child or grandson. (153–54).

The grandmother has arranged to meet Libor solely in order to ask him, as a one-time writer about show business luminaries, to speak out against the famous film director who declared that he "understood" why the Algerian blinded her grandson: "Because of Gaza, he says he understands why people hate Jews and want to kill them."

The moviemaker goes unnamed but he is almost certainly based upon Ken Loach. A Trotskyist, Loach collaborated with author Jim Allen to produce the "poisonously" (thus Arnold Wesker) antisemitic play *Perdition*, which depicted the Holocaust as the product of a Zionist-Nazi conspiracy. We do not learn until nearly the end of the book that Libor fails Emmy because he too had succumbed to the anti-Jewish tsunami, now so powerful in England that both the Jew Finkler and the non-Jew Treslove discover that they have produced antisemitic sons. Libor's apparent Zionism had been no more than "lifeboat" Zionism, a place of refuge when Europe returned to its default ideology. By the time Emmy asks for his help against the moral desperadoes of England's artistic/learned classes, he has decided that the Jews must disappear: "I will have no more Jews." And he practices what he preaches, committing suicide in Eastbourne.

The Finkler Question is not quite the literary masterpiece that numerous reviewers have declared it to be. It is full of verbal tics, small jokes that are amusing when first told but become cloying by the fourth or fifth repetition, and resort to words (like "methodology") that usually betray a virgin mind seduced by the temptation of a few extra syllables into saying what the writer does not mean. Nevertheless, the work has what John Ruskin called "noble imperfection" and a great truth-telling power.

The last few pages of this *comic* novel include the following: the suicide of Libor; a somber gathering at his grave in London; the near lynching of a Sephardic Jewish boy in Regent's Park; the opening of a Museum of Anglo-Jewish Culture in St. John's Wood attended by twelve people, a greater number of anti-Israel demonstrators led by "the Jew in the PLO scarf," and watchful police; a recitation of the *Kaddish*. The very English Jacobson appears to have adopted the wise slogan of his cross-channel neighbors: *Il faut rire pour ne pas pleurer.*

Notes

1. Howard Jacobson, *The Finkler Question* (New York: Bloomsbury, 2010), 162, 195. Subsequent references to this work will be given in parentheses in the text.
2. On Judt, see *The Jewish Divide over Israel: Accusers and Defenders*, ed. Edward Alexander and Paul Bogdanor (New Brunswick, NJ: Transaction Publishers, 2006), xv and 65–71.
3. On Rose, see Benjamin Balint's essay, "What Zionism Is Not," *Weekly Standard*, November 14, 2005.

12

Israelis against Themselves: The Intellectual Origins of Oslo and Intifada II (2006)

> "When it comes to defaming Jews, the Palestinians
> are *pisherkes* next to *Ha'aretz*."
> —Philip Roth *(Operation Shylock, 1991)*

I

In his essay of 1838 on Jeremy Bentham, John Stuart Mill wrote that "speculative philosophy, which to the superficial appears a thing so remote from the business of life and the outward interests of men, is in reality the thing on earth which most influences them, and in the long run overbears every other influence save those which it must itself obey." Of course Mill was not always willing to wait for the long run and was often tempted by shortcuts whereby speculative philosophers and other intellectuals could make their influence felt upon government. Frightened by Tocqueville's observations of American democracy, Mill sought to prevent the "tyranny of the majority" by an elaborate scheme of plural voting that would give everybody one vote but intellectuals a larger number; when he awoke to the folly and danger of such a scheme, he switched his allegiance to proportional representation as a means of allowing what he calls in *On Liberty* the wise and noble few to exercise their due influence over the mindless majority.

By now we have had enough experience of the influence of intellectuals in politics to be skeptical of Mill's schemes. To look back over the major American intellectual journals in the years prior to and during the Second World War—not only Trotskyist publications like *New International* or Dwight Macdonald's *Politics*, but the highbrow modernist and Marxist *Partisan Review*—is to be appalled by the spectacle of the finest minds of America vociferous in opposition to prosecuting the war against Hitler, which in their view was just a parochial struggle between two dying capitalist forces. The pacifism of English intellectuals in the late thirties led George Orwell to declare that some ideas are so stupid that only intellectuals could believe them; and in one of his *Tribune* columns of 1943, he said of the left-wing rumor in London that America had entered the war only in order to crush a budding English socialist revolution that "one has to belong to the intelligentsia to believe something like that. No ordinary man could be such a fool."

If we look at the influence of Israeli intellectuals upon Israeli policy over the decades, and especially during the Yitzhak Rabin/Shimon Peres and Ehud Barak governments that prepared the Oslo Accords (1993, 1995) and, by 2000, Intifada II, we may conclude that Mill and Orwell were both right, Mill in stressing the remarkable power of ideas, Orwell in insisting that such power often works evil, not good.

Among the numerous misfortunes that have beset the Zionist enterprise from its inception—the unyielding hardness of the land allegedly flowing with milk and honey, the failure of the Jews of the Diaspora to move to Zion except under duress, the constant burden of peril arising from Arab racism and imperialism—was the premature birth of an intellectual class, especially a literary intelligentsia. The quality of Israel's intelligentsia may be a matter of dispute. Gershom Scholem once remarked, mischievously, that talent goes where it is needed, and in Israel it was needed far more urgently in the military than in the universities, the literary community, the arts, and journalism. But the influence of this intelligentsia is less open to dispute than its quality. When Shimon Peres (who views himself as an intellectual) launched his ill-fated election campaign of spring 1996, he surrounded himself with artists and intellectuals on the stage of Tel Aviv's Mann Auditorium.[1] Three months earlier he had listed as one of the three future stars of the Labor Party the internationally famous novelist Amos Oz, the same Amos Oz who was notorious among religiously observant Jewish "settlers" for having referred to their organization Gush Emunim (Block of the Faithful) in a speech of June 1989 in language generally reserved for thieves and murderers: they were, he told a Peace Now gathering of about 20,000 people in Tel Aviv's Malchei Yisrael Square, "a small sect, a messianic sect, obtuse and cruel, [who] emerged a few years ago from a dark corner of Judaism, and [are] threatening to . . . impose on us a wild and insane blood ritual. . . . They are guilty of crimes against humanity."

Intellectuals in many countries have adopted the motto: "the *other* country, right or wrong," and worked mightily to undermine national confidence in their country's heritage, founding principles, *raison d'être*. But such intellectuals do not usually arise within fifty years of their country's founding, and in no case except Israel have intellectuals cultivated their "alienation" in a country whose "right to exist" is considered an acceptable subject of discussion among otherwise respectable people and nations. As Midge Decter shrewdly put it in May 1996, "A country only half a century old is not supposed to have a full fledged accomplished literary intelligentsia.... This is an extravagance only an old and stable country should be allowed to indulge in."[2]

The seeds of trouble amongst intellectuals in Zion antedated the state itself. On May Day 1936 the Labor Zionist leader Berl Katznelson asked, angrily,

> Is there another people on earth whose sons are so emotionally and mentally twisted that they consider everything their nation does despicable and hateful, while every murder, rape and robbery committed by their enemies fills their hearts with admiration and awe? As long as a Jewish child ... can come to the Land of Israel, and here catch the virus of self-hate ... let not our conscience be still.[3]

But what for Katznelson was a sick aberration would later become the normal condition among a substantial segment of Israeli intellectuals. A major turning point came in 1967, when the doctors of Israel's soul, a numerous fraternity, concluded that in winning a defensive war that, if lost, would have brought its destruction, Israel had bartered its soul for a piece of land. The Arab nations, shrewdly sensing that Jews were far less capable of waging the war of ideas than the war of planes and tanks, quickly transformed the rhetoric of their opposition to Israel's existence from the right to the left, from the aspiration to "turn the Mediterranean red with Jewish blood" (the battle cry of the months preceding the Six-Day War) to the pretended search for a haven for the homeless. This calculated appeal to liberals, as Ruth Wisse has amply demonstrated,[4] created legions of critics of the Jewish state, especially among devout believers in the progressive improvement and increasing enlightenment of the human race. Israeli intellectuals who were willing to express, especially in dramatic hyperbole, criticism of their own country's alleged racism, imperialism, and religious fanaticism quickly became celebrities in the American press. They were exalted by people like Anthony Lewis as courageous voices of dissent, even though what they had joined was just the opposite: a community of *con*sent.

But it was not until a decade later that the Israeli intelligentsia turned massively against the state, against Zionism, against Judaism itself. For in 1977 the Labor Party lost its twenty-nine-year-old ownership of government to people it considered its cultural inferiors, people Meron Benvenisti described as follows: "I remember traveling on a Haifa bus and looking around at my fellow passengers with contempt and indifference—almost as lower forms of human life."[5] Such hysteria (which burst forth again in May 1996 when Benjamin Netanyahu won the election) now became the standard pose of the alienated Israeli intellectual, and it was aggressively disseminated by American publications such as the *New York Times*, ever eager for Israeli-accented confirmation of its own views. Amos Oz, for example, took to the pages of the *New York Times Magazine* during the Lebanon War to deplore the imminent demise of Israel's "soul": "Israel could have become an exemplary state . . . a small-scale laboratory for democratic socialism." But that great hope, Oz lamented, was dashed by the arrival of Holocaust refugees, various "anti-socialist" Zionists, "chauvinistic, militaristic, and xenophobic" North African Jews, and so forth.[6] (These are essentially the reasons why it was not until Menachem Begin became prime minister that the Ethiopian Jews could come to Israel.) By 1995 Oz was telling *New York Times* readers that supporters of the Likud party were accomplices of Hamas.[7] Even after spiritual brethren of Hamas massacred three thousand people in the United States on September 11, 2001, Oz declared that the enemy was not in any sense the radical Islamist or Arabic mentality but simply "fanaticism," and that in any case the most pressing matter he could think of was to give "Palestinians their natural right to self-determination." For good measure he added the patently false assertion that "almost all [Moslems] are as shocked and aggrieved [by the suicide bombings of America] as the rest of mankind."[8] Apparently Oz had missed all those photos of Muslims round the world handing out candy, ululating, dancing, and jubilating over dead Jews and dead Americans. It was a remarkable performance, which made one wonder whether Oz gets to write about politics because he is a novelist or gets his reputation as a novelist because of his political views.

People like Benvenisti—sociologist, deputy mayor of Jerusalem until fired by Teddy Kollek, and favorite authority on Israel for many years of the *New York Times* and *New York Review of Books*—foreshadowed the boasting of the intellectual spokesmen of later Labor governments that they were not only post-Zionist but also post-Jewish in their thinking. Benvenisti, writing in 1987, recalled proudly how "we would observe Yom Kippur by loading quantities of food onto a raft and swimming out with it to an offshore islet in the Mediterranean, and there we would while away the whole day feasting. It was a flagrant demonstration of our rejection of religious and Diaspora values."[9]

Anecdotal evidence of the increasingly shrill anti-Israelism (or worse) of Israeli intellectuals is only too easy to amass. The sculptor Yigal Tumarkin once stated that "when I see the black-coated *haredim* with the children they spawn, I can understand the Holocaust."[10] Ze'ev Sternhell, Hebrew University expert on fascism, proposed destroying the Jewish settlements with IDF tanks as a means of boosting national morale.[11] In 1969 the guru of Labor Party intellectuals, the late Professor Yeshayahu Leibowitz, began to talk of the inevitable "Nazification" of the Israeli nation and society. By the time of the Lebanon War, he had become an international celebrity because of his use of the epithet "Judeo-Nazi" to describe the Israeli army. When Iraq invaded Kuwait in 1990, he outdid even himself by declaring (in words redolent of what Katznelson had deplored in 1936): "Everything Israel has done, and I emphasize *everything*, in the past 23 years is either evil stupidity or stupidly evil."[12] And in 1993 Leibowitz would be honored by the government of Yitzhak Rabin with the Israel Prize.

In third place after Oz and Benvenisti among the resources of intellectual insight into Israel's soul frequently mined over the years by Anthony Lewis, Thomas Friedman, and like-minded journalists is David Grossman, the novelist. Grossman established his credentials as an alienated intellectual commentator on the state of his country's mind in a book of 1988 called *The Yellow Wind*, an account of his seven-week journey through the "West Bank," a journey undertaken in order to understand "how an entire nation like mine, an enlightened nation by all accounts, is able to train itself to live as a conqueror without making its own life wretched."[13] This is a complicated book, not without occasional patches of honesty. But its true flavor can be suggested by two successive chapters dealing with culture and books, especially religious ones. Grossman first visits the Jewish settlement of Ofra, at which he arrives fully armed with suspicion, hostility, and partisanship, a "wary stranger" among people who remind him, he says, of nothing human, especially when they are "in the season of their messianic heat" (52). In Ofra, Grossman does not want "to let down his guard" and be "seduced" by the Sabbath "warmth" and "festivity"

of these wily Jews (34). Although most of his remarks to Arabs in conversation recounted in *The Yellow Wind* are the perfunctory gestures
of a straight man to whom his interlocutors pay no serious attention,
he angrily complains that the Jewish settlers don't listen to or "display a
real interest" in him. He asks them to "imagine themselves in their Arab
neighbors' places" (37) and is very much the angry schoolmaster when
they don't act like compliant puppets or accept his pretense that this
act of sympathetic imagination is devoid of political meaning. Neither
are the settlers intellectually nimble enough to make the appropriate
reply to Grossman: "My dear fellow, we will imagine ourselves as Arabs
if you will imagine yourself as a Jew." But Grossman has no intention
of suspending his own rhythms of existence long enough to penetrate
the inner life of these alien people: "What have I to do with them?"
(48). His resentment is as much cultural as political. He complains that
the settlers have "little use for culture," speak bad Hebrew, indulge in
"Old Diaspora type" humor, and own no books, "with the exception
of religious texts" (46). And these, far from mitigating the barbarity
of their owners, aggravate it. The final image of the Jews in this long
chapter is of "potential [!] terrorists now rocking over their books" (51).
For Grossman the conjectural terrorism of Jews is a far more grievous
matter than the actual terrorism of Arabs.

The following chapter also treats of culture and books, including
religious ones. Grossman has come to Bethlehem University, one of
several universities in the territories that have been punningly described
as branches of PLO state. Here Grossman, though he admits the school
to be "a stronghold of the Democratic Front for the Liberation of Palestine," sees no terrorists rocking over books, but rather idyllic scenes that
remind him of "the pictures of Plato's school in Athens" (57). Bubbling
with affection, eager to ascribe only the highest motives, Grossman is
now willing to forgive even readers of religious books. He has not so
much as a snort or a sneer for the Bethlehem English professor who
ascribes Arabs' supreme sensitivity to lyric rhythm in English poetry to
the "rhythm of the Koran flow[ing] through their blood" (59). The author's
ability to spot racism at a distance of twenty miles when he is among
Jews slackens when timeless racial categories are invoked in Bethlehem.

When the Labor Party returned to power in 1992, so too did the
Israeli intellectuals and their disciples. People once (rather naively)
casually referred to as extremists moved to the centers of power in
Israeli government and policy formation. Dedi Zucker, who used to
accuse Jewish settlers of drinking blood on Passover; Yossi Sarid,

who once shocked Israelis by declaring that Holocaust Memorial Day meant nothing to him; and Shulamit Aloni, whose statements about religious Jews would probably have landed her in jail in European countries that have laws against antisemitic provocation, all became cabinet ministers or prominent spokesmen in the government of Rabin. Two previously obscure professors laid the foundations for the embrace of Yasser Arafat, one of the major war criminals of the twentieth century, responsible for the murder of more Jews than anyone since Hitler and Stalin. The Oslo process put the PLO well on the way to an independent Palestinian state, had Arafat, or any other Arab leaders, actually desired one. Amos Oz and A. B. Yehoshua and David Grossman were delighted. Oz announced in 1993 that "death shall be no more," and Grossman assured Anthony Lewis that Israel had finally given up its "instinctive suspicion," and that although "we have the worst terrorism," "we are making peace."[14] Benvenisti proved harder to satisfy: in 1995 he published a book called *Intimate Enemies*, the ads for which carried glowing endorsements from Thomas Friedman and Professor Ian Lustick, in which he proposed dissolution of the state of Israel.

Only a few figures within Israel's cultural establishment expressed dismay at what was happening. The philosopher Eliezer Schweid warned that a nation that starts by abandoning its cultural memories ends by abandoning its physical existence.[15] Amos Perlmutter analyzed the "post-Zionism" of Israeli academics as an all-out attack on the validity of the state.[16] A still more notable exception to the general euphoria of this class was Aharon Megged. In June 1994 this well-known writer and longtime supporter of the Labor Party wrote an explosive article in *Ha'aretz* on "The Israeli Suicide Drive" in which he connected the Rabin government's record of endless unreciprocated concessions to a PLO that had not even canceled its charter calling for Israel's destruction, to the self-destructiveness that had long before infected Israel's intellectual classes. "Since the Six Day War," Megged wrote, "and at an increasing pace, we have witnessed a phenomenon which probably has no parallel in history: an emotional and moral identification by the majority of Israel's intelligentsia with people openly committed to our annihilation." Megged argued that since 1967 the Israeli intelligentsia had more and more come "to regard religious, cultural, and emotional affinity to the land . . . with sheer contempt"; and he observed that the equation of Israelis with Nazis had become an article of faith and the central idea of "*thousands* [emphasis added] of articles and reports in the press, hundreds of poems . . . dozens of documentary and feature films, exhibitions and paintings and photos." He also shrewdly remarked on the methods by which anti-Zionist Israeli intellectuals disseminated their message and reputations. Writers like Benny Morris, Ilan Pappe, and Baruch Kimmerling "mostly publish first in English to gain the praise of the West's 'justice seekers.' Their works are then quickly translated into Arabic and displayed in Damascus, Cairo and Tunis. Their conclusion is almost uniform: that in practice Zionism amounts to an evil, colonialist conspiracy."[17]

The minds of the majority of those who carried on the Oslo Process of the Israeli government from 1993 to 1996 were formed by the writers, artists, and publicists whom Megged excoriated. Although Shimon Peres's utterances about the endless war for independence that his country has been forced to wage often seemed to come from a man who had taken leave of the actual world, they were rooted in the "post-Zionist," post-Jewish, and universalist assumptions of the Israeli intelligentsia. Just as they were contemptuous of any tie with the land of Israel, so he repeatedly alleged that land plays no part in Judaism or even in the Jewish political philosophy that names itself after a specific mountain called Zion. Like the Israeli intelligentsia, he accused Israel's religious Jews of an atavistic attachment to territory over "spirit," claiming that Judaism is "ethical/moral and spiritual, and not an idolatry of soil-worship."[18] Just as Israeli intellectuals nimbly pursued and imitated the latest cultural fads of America and Europe, hoping to be assimilated by the great world outside Israel, so did Peres hope that Israel would one day be admitted into the Arab League.[19]

Despite the enlistment of then President William Clinton as virtually his campaign manager, and the nearly unanimous support he received from the Israeli and world news media, to say nothing of the herd of independent thinkers from the universities, and the rented academics of the think tanks, Shimon Peres and his Oslo Process were decisively rejected by the Jewish voters of Israel. Predictably, the Israeli intellectuals (not guessing that Labor's successors would blindly continue the process) reacted with melodramatic hysteria. David Grossman, in the *New York Times* of May 31, wailed sanctimoniously that "Israel has moved toward the extreme right . . . more militant, more religious, more fundamentalist, more tribal and more racist."[20]

Among the American liberal supporters of Israel's intellectual elite, only the *New Republic* appeared somewhat chastened by the election result. Having for years, perhaps decades, celebrated the ineffable genius of Shimon Peres and his coterie, the magazine turned angrily upon the Israeli intellectuals for failing to grasp that "their association with Peres was one of the causes of his defeat."

> Disdainful of [Jews] from traditional communities, they thought of and called such people "stupid Sephardim." This contempt for Arab Jews expresses itself in a cruel paradox, for it coexists with a credulity about, and esteem for, the Middle East's Christians and Muslims—Arab Arabs. Such esteem, coupled with a derisive attitude toward Jewish symbols and texts, rituals, remembrances and anxieties, sent tens of thousands to Netanyahu.[21]

II

The most ambitious attempt to trace the history and analyze the causes of the maladies of Israeli intellectuals is Yoram Hazony's book *The Jewish State*, which appeared early in the year 2000. Within months of its publication, the dire consequences of the Oslo Accords, post-Zionism's major political achievement, became visible to everybody in Israel in the form of Intifada II, otherwise known as the Oslo War, a campaign of unremitting atrocities—pogroms, lynchings, suicide bombings—launched by Yasser Arafat after 97% of his demands, including an independent Palestinian state, had been conceded by the government of the hapless Ehud Barak.

The Jewish State: The Struggle for Israel's Soul is a broadside aimed at those Israelis who, in what its author calls "a carnival of self-loathing,"[22] are busily eating away at the Jewish foundations of that state. The book's very title is a conscious affront to Israel's *branja*, a slang term for the "progressive" and "enlightened" experts whose views, according to Supreme Court Chief Justice Aharon Barak, should determine the court's decisions on crucial matters. For these *illuminati* have sought to enlist no less a figure than Theodor Herzl in their campaign to de-Judaize the state of Israel. Nearly all the "post-Zionists" discussed in *The Jewish State* claim that Herzl did not intend the title of his famous book to be *The Jewish State* at all, that the state he proposed was in no significant sense intrinsically Jewish, and that he believed in a total separation of religion from the state. Hazony argues (and massively demonstrates) that Herzl believed a Jewish state was essential to rescue the Jewish people from both antisemitism and assimilation, the forces that were destroying Jewish life throughout the Diaspora. (Most of Herzl's rabbinic opponents argued that Zionism was itself but a thinly veiled form of assimilation.)

Hazony's *Jewish State* has two purposes. The first is to show that "the idea of the Jewish state is under systematic attack from its own cultural and intellectual establishment" (xxvii). These "culture makers" have not only renounced the idea of a Jewish state—"A state," claims Amos Oz, "cannot be Jewish, just as a chair or a bus cannot be Jewish" (338). The writers who dominate Israeli culture, Hazony argues, are adept at imagining what it is like to be an Arab; they have, like the aforementioned David Grossman, much more trouble imagining what it is like to be a Jew.

If Israeli intellectuals were merely supplying their own illustration of Orwell's quip about the unique susceptibility of intellectuals to stupid ideas, their hostility to Israel's Jewish traditions and Zionist character would not merit much concern. But Hazony shows that they have had spectacular success, amounting to a virtual coup d'état, in their political struggle for a post-Jewish state. "What is perhaps most remarkable about the advance of the new ideas in Israeli government policy is the way in which even the most sweeping changes in Israel's character as a Jewish state can be effected by a handful of intellectuals, with only the most minimal of opposition from the country's political leaders or the public" (52).

The post-Zionists imposed their views in the public-school curriculum, in the Basic Laws of the country, and in the IDF (Israel Defense Force), whose code of ethics now excluded any allusion to Jewish or Zionist principles. The author of the code was Asa Kasher, one of Israel's most enterprising post-Zionists, who modestly described his composition as "the most profound code of ethics in the world of military ethics, in particular, and in the world of professional ethics, in general"—so terminally profound, in fact, that an Israeli soldier "doesn't need to think or philosophize anymore. Someone else already . . . did the thinking and decided. There are no dilemmas" (53, 56).

The ultimate triumph of post-Zionism, Hazony argues, came in its conquest of the Foreign Ministry and the mind of Shimon Peres. Both came to the conclusion that Israel must retreat from the idea of an independent Jewish state. In the accord reached with Egypt in 1978 and even in the 1994 accord with Jordan, Israeli governments had insisted that the Arab signatories recognize the Jewish state's "sovereignty, territorial integrity, and political independence" (58). But the Oslo accords with the fanatically anti-Zionist PLO conceded on every one of these issues; and if the agreement with the PLO was partly an effect of post-Zionism, it was an effect that became in turn a cause—giving respectability and wide exposure to post-Zionist political prejudices formerly confined to coteries in Rehavia and Ramat-Aviv.

Thereafter, Peres and his Foreign Office routinely promoted the interests not of a sovereign Jewish state but of the (largely Arab) Middle East. In a reversal of policy akin to that of the Soviet Foreign Ministry in the wake of Stalin's pact with Hitler, Uri Savir and other Foreign Ministry officials exhorted American Jews who had for decades resisted the Arab campaign to blacken Israel's reputation to support U.S. foreign aid to the two chief blackeners, the PLO and Syria. They—it was alleged—needed dollars much more than Israel. Peres himself, as we observed earlier, carried the post-Zionist campaign for assimilation and universalism to the global level, grandly announcing in December 1994 that "Israel's next goal should be to become a member of the Arab League" (67).

The second part of Hazony's book has a twofold purpose. The first is to write the history of the ideological and political struggle within the Jewish world itself over the idea of the Jewish state, paying particular attention to how that ideal, which a few decades ago had been axiomatic among virtually all Jews the world over, had so quickly "been brought to ruin among the cultural leadership of the Jewish state itself" (78). Hazony's second aim as historian is to demonstrate the power of ideas, especially the truth of J. S. Mill's axiom about the practical potency, in the long run, of (apparently useless) speculative philosophy. It was the power of ideas that enabled philosopher Martin Buber and other opponents of the Jewish state to break Ben-Gurion and to undermine the practical-minded stalwarts of Labor Zionism. (Likud hardly figures in this book. The quarrels between Ben-Gurion and Begin have from Hazony's perspective "the character of a squabble between the captain and the first mate of a sinking ship" [79].)

Hazony is a masterful political and cultural historian, and his fascinating account of the long struggle of Buber (and his Hebrew University acolytes) against Herzl and Ben-Gurion's conception of a genuinely Jewish state is told with tremendous verve and insight. Buber is at once the villain and the hero of this book. He is the villain in his relentless opposition to a Jewish state; in his licentious equations between Labor Zionists and Nazis; in his fierce anti-(Jewish) immigration stance (announced the day after he himself had immigrated from Germany in 1938). But he is the hero because his posthumous ideological victory over Labor Zionism—most of today's leading post-Zionists claim that their minds were formed by Buber and his binationalist Brit Shalom/Ihud allies at Hebrew University—is in Hazony's view the most stunning example of how ideas and myths are in the long run of more political importance than kibbutzim and settlements. Because Buber understood the way in which culture eventually determines politics and grasped the potency of books and journals and (most of all) universities, his (to Hazony) malignant influence now carries the day in Israel's political as well as its cultural wars.

Hazony argues that since the fall of Ben-Gurion, Israel has had no prime minister—not Golda Meir, not Menachem Begin—who was an "idea-maker." Even the very shrewd Ben-Gurion and Berl Katznelson (who presciently warned of the dangers lurking in the "intellectual famine" [299] of Labor Israel) were slow to recognize the potentially disastrous consequences of entrusting the higher education of their children to a university largely controlled (for twenty-four years) by the anti-Zionist Judah Magnes and largely staffed by faculty he recruited. Magnes, in language foreshadowing the clichés of today's post-Zionists, charged that the Jewish settlement in Palestine had been "born in sin" (203); moreover, he believed that seeing history from the Arabs' historical perspective was one of the main reasons for establishing the Hebrew University.

Hazony's book is written backward, something like a murder mystery. He begins with a dismaying, indeed terrifying picture of a nearly moribund people, exhausted, confused, aimless—their traditional Labor Zionist assumptions declared "effectively dead" by their formerly Labor Zionist leaders, most crucially Shimon Peres. He then moves backward to seek the reasons why the Zionist enterprise is in danger of being dismantled, not by Israel's Arab enemies (who gleefully watch the spectacle unfold), but by its own heavily petted intellectual, artistic, and political elite—professors, writers, luminaries in the visual arts.

The material in the early chapters is shocking, and I speak as one who thought he had seen it all: the visiting sociologist from Hebrew University who adorned his office at my university with a PLO recruiting poster; the Tel Aviv University philosophy professor who supplied Noam Chomsky's supporters with a letter of kashrut certifying the "lifelong dedication to Israel" of their (Israel-hating) idol; the Haifa University sociologist active in the American-Arab Anti-Discrimination League (a PLO front group); the contingent of Israeli professors taking up arms on behalf of the great prevaricator Edward Said. But the material Hazony collected (and dissected) from Israel's post-Zionist and post-Jewish intellectuals continues to shock nevertheless. Compared with the Baruch Kimmerlings, the Asa Kashers, the Ilan Pappes, and other protagonists in Hazony's tragedy, Austria's Jorge Haider, the right-wing demagogue about whom the Israeli government once kicked up such a fuss, is a Judeophile and lover of Zion.

Hazony carefully refrains from applying the term "antisemitic" to even the most extreme defamations of Jewish tradition and of the Jewish state by post-Zionists and their epigones. But surely such reticence is unnecessary when the secret has long been out. As far back as May 1987, the Israeli humorist and cartoonist Dosh, in a column in *Ma'ariv*, drew a picture of a shopper in a store that specialized in antisemitic merchandise reaching for the top shelf—on which lay the most expensive item, adorned by a *Stuermer*-like caricature of a Jew and prominently labelled "Made in Israel." The article this cartoon illustrated spoke of Israel's need to increase exports by embellishing products available elsewhere in the world with unique local characteristics. Israel had done this with certain fruits and vegetables in the past, and now it was doing the same with defamations of Israel, produced in Israel. Customers were getting more selective, no longer willing to make do with grade B merchandise produced by British leftists or French neo-Nazis. No, they wanted authentic material, from local sources; and Israeli intellectuals, artists, playwrights, were responding with alacrity to the opportunity.

But Dosh had spoken merely of a specialty shop. To accommodate the abundant production of Hazony's gallery of post-Zionist/post-Jewish defamers of Israel (both the people and the land) would require a department store twice the size of Macy's or Harrod's. On bargain day, one imagines the following recitation by the elevator operator: "First floor, Moshe Zimmermann, Yeshayahu Leibowitz, and sixty-eight other members of the progressive and universalist community on Israelis as Nazis; second floor, A. B. Yehoshua on the need for Israeli Jews to become 'normal' by converting to Christianity or Islam; third floor, Boaz Evron in justification of Vichy France's anti-Jewish measures; fourth floor, Idith Zertal on Zionist absorption of Holocaust refugees as a form of rape; fifth floor, Benny Morris on Zionism as ethnic cleansing; attic, Shulamit Aloni on Zionism (also Judaism) as racism; basement, Ya'akov Yovel justifying the medieval blood libel; sub-basement, Yigal Tumarkin justifying Nazi murder of (religious) Jews. Watch your step, please."

Although Hazony's argument for the large role played by Israel's professoriat in dismantling Labor Zionism is convincing, it cannot be a sufficient cause of current post-Zionism and post-Judaism. The habitual language of post-Zionists, and most especially their hammering insistence on the contradiction between being Jewish and being human, is exactly the language of European Jewish ideologues of assimilation over a century ago. Gidon Samet, one of the numerous resident ideologues of post-Judaism and post-Zionism at *Ha'aretz*, is not far from the truth when he likens their attractions to those of American junk food and junk music: "Madonna and Big Macs," Samet says, "are only the most peripheral of examples" of the wonderful blessings of Israel's new "normalness" (71–72). Of course, whatever we may think of those who in 1900 urged fellow Jews to cease being Jewish in order to join universal humanity, they at least were not promoting this sinister distinction in full knowledge of how it would be used by Hitler; the same cannot be said of contemporary Israeli ideologues of assimilation and universalism.

Most readers of post-Zionist outpourings have little to fall back on except their native mistrust of intellectuals. Thus when Hebrew University professor Moshe Zimmermann declares that Zionism "imported" antisemitism into the Middle East (11), it requires knowledge (not much, to be sure) of history to recognize the statement as preposterous. But sometimes the post-Zionists are tripped up by overconfidence into lies that even the uninstructed can easily detect. Thus Avishai Margalit, a Hebrew University philosophy professor spiritually close to, if not quite a card-carrying member of, the post-Zionists, in a *New York Review of Books* essay of 1988 called "The Kitsch of Israel," heaped scorn upon the "children's room" at Yad Vashem with its "tape-recorded voices of children crying out in Yiddish, 'Mame, Tate [Mother, Father].'" Yad Vashem is a favorite target of the post-Zionists because they believe it encourages Jews to think not only that they were singled out for annihilation by the Nazis but also—how unreasonable of them!—to want to make sure they do not get singled out for destruction again. But, as any Jerusalemite or tourist who can get over to Mount Herzl will quickly discover, there is no "children's room" and there are no taped voices at Yad Vashem. There is a memorial to the murdered children and a tape-recorded voice that reads their names.[23] Margalit's skullduggery is by no means the worst of its kind among those Israelis involved in derogating the memory and history of the country's Jewish population. But it comes as no surprise to learn from Hazony that Margalit believes Israel is morally obligated to offer Arabs "special rights" for the protection of their culture and to be "neutral" toward the Jews (13). With such neutrality as Margalit's, who needs belligerence?

In Hazony Israel had perhaps found its latter-day Jeremiah, but given the widespread tone deafness of the country's enlightened classes to their Jewish heritage, perhaps what is needed at the moment is an Israeli Jonathan Swift, especially the Swift who in his versified will "gave the little wealth he had / To build a house for fools and mad; / And showed by one satiric touch, / No nation wanted it so much."

I began this essay with statements by J. S. Mill and George Orwell about the role of intellectuals and their ideas in politics, and I shall conclude in the same way. The first statement, by Mill, might usefully be recommended as an aid to reflection by the intellectuals of Israel: "The collective mind," wrote Mill in 1838, "does not penetrate below the surface, but it sees all the surface; which profound thinkers, even by reason of their profundity, often fail to do." The second statement, by Orwell, seems particularly relevant as the Arab Muslim war against Israel rages on, unabated: "If the radical intellectuals in England had had their way in the 20's and 30's," said Orwell, "the Gestapo would have been walking the streets of London in 1940."[24]

Notes

1. *Jerusalem Post*, April 6, 1996.
2. Midge Decter, "The Treason of the Intellectuals," *Outpost*, May 1996, 7.
3. *Kitvei B. Katznelson* (Tel Aviv: Workers' Party of Israel, 1961), 8:18.
4. Ruth R. Wisse, *If I Am Not for Myself . . . The Liberal Betrayal of the Jews* (New York: Free Press, 1992).
5. Meron Benvenisti, *Conflicts and Contradictions* (New York: Villard, 1986), 70.
6. *New York Times Magazine*, July 11, 1982.
7. *New York Times*, April 11, 1995.
8. "Struggling against Fanaticism," *New York Times*, September 14, 2001.
9. Benvenisti, *Conflicts*, 34.
10. *Jerusalem Post*, December 1, 1990.
11. Ibid.
12. *Jerusalem Post*, January 16, 1993.
13. *The Yellow Wind*, trans. Haim Watzman (New York: Farrar, Straus & Giroux, 1988), 212. Subsequent references to this work will be cited in text.
14. *New York Times*, May 17, 1996. The most detailed account of the influence of Israeli intellectuals specifically on the Oslo Accords is Kenneth Levin, *The Oslo Syndrome: Delusions of a People under Siege* (Hanover, NH: Smith and Kraus Global, 2005).
15. *Jerusalem Post International Edition*, April 15, 1995.
16. "Egalitarians Gone Mad," *Jerusalem Post International Edition*, October 28, 1995.
17. Aharon Megged, "The Israeli Suicide Drive," *Jerusalem Post International Edition*, July 2, 1994.
18. Quoted in Moshe Kohn, "Check Your Quotes," *Jerusalem Post International Edition*, October 16, 1993.

19. The Arab League contemptuously replied that Israel could become a member only "after the complete collapse of the Zionist national myth, and the complete conversion of historical Palestine into one democratic state to which all the Palestinians will return."

20. "The Fortress Within," *New York Times*, May 31, 1996.

21. "Revolt of the Masses," *New Republic*, June 24, 1996.

22. *The Jewish State: The Struggle for Israel's Soul* (New York: Basic Books, 2000), 339. Subsequent references to this work will be cited in parentheses in the text.

23. Ten years later Margalit reprinted this piece in a collection of his essays called *Views in Review*. There he says he has omitted a sentence from the original essay that "had wrong information in it about the children's memorial room at Yad Vashem." But he blames this on "an employee" who misled him. Margalit's sleight of hand here reveals two things: (1) When he says in his introduction to the book that "I am not even an eyewitness to much of what I write about," we can believe him. (2) The Yiddish writer Shmuel Niger was correct to say that "we suffer not only from Jews who are too coarse, but also from Jews who are too sensitive."

24. In *The Lion and the Unicorn* (1941), Orwell also wrote, "The really important fact about the English intelligentsia is their severance from the common culture of the country. . . . In the general patriotism, they form an island of dissident thought. England is the only great nation whose intellectuals are ashamed of their country." This, not to put too fine a point upon it, no longer seems true.

13

Jewish Israel-Haters Convert Their Dead Grandmothers: A New Mormonism? (2012)

> "Who is a Jew? A Jew is someone with Jewish grandchildren."
> —Yosef Haim Brenner

In February 2012 Elie Wiesel asked Mitt Romney to urge his Mormon coreligionists (members of the Church of Jesus Christ of Latter-Day Saints) to repudiate their practice of "proxy" baptism requests for Holocaust victims, including Wiesel's own ancestors. Jews have long objected to the Mormon practice of "vicariously" converting their deceased ancestors, especially those who perished in the Holocaust, to the Mormon faith, a practice that has seemed to them more brazenly dogmatic than the worst excesses of the Inquisition. But now it seems that Jewish Israel-haters, people who define their "Jewishness" almost entirely by their repudiation of the Jewish state, have developed their own brand of Mormonism. It consists of converting deceased Zionist grandparents (especially of the female sort) to their own pseudo-religion, which starts from the premise that when a person can no longer be a Jew, he (or she) becomes an anti-Zionist.

In the December 21, 2010, issue of the *National Post* (Canada), the astute journalist Barbara Kay expressed the hope that "after I have shuffled off this mortal coil, none of my granddaughters will turn into useful idiots for a rotten political movement riddled with antisemitism." Kay was alluding to two unusually foul volleys of fire and vitriol shot in the direction of Israel and her Jewish supporters by Canadian Jewish women, Jennifer Peto and Judy Rebick.

Peto, a twenty-nine-year-old activist on behalf of lesbian and anti-Zionist causes (sometimes happily intermarried as "Queers against Israel") has gained notoriety for a master's thesis with the bombastic title ("The Victimhood of the Powerful: White Jews, Zionism and the Racism of Hegemonic Holocaust Education"), submitted to and approved by the "sociology and equity" cranny of a minor nook of the University of Toronto called Ontario Institute of Studies in Education (OISE). In its regurgitation of hoary antisemitic tropes directed at "Jewish privilege," "Jewish racism," and the "apartheid" state of Israel, the thesis reminded many of the pseudo-scholarly materials studied (and brilliantly dissected) in Max Weinreich's *Hitler's Professors* (1946), a book that showed how German academics were the first to make antisemitism both academically respectable and complicit in murder.

Peto's malice toward and ignorance about Jews and Israel know no bounds. Jews who wish to remember the Holocaust are "racists" (an epithet without which she would be hard pressed to speak) who want to monopolize all that beautiful suffering that other groups would very much like, *ex post facto*, to share. Israel, not only a country in which Arabs and Jews share the same buses, beaches, clinics, cafes, soccer pitches, and universities, but the only country in history to have brought thousands of black people to its shores to become citizens and not slaves, is for her the quintessentially "apartheid" state. Chief among the multifarious abominations that Peto imputes to the wily Jews is "Hegemonic Holocaust Education." Professor Werner Cohn, the first to call attention to the scandal of Peto's thesis (and the still greater scandal that her academic adviser, one Sheryl Nestel, routinely encourages and approves such theses), noted that Peto uses the word "hegemonic," with hammering insistence, fifty-two times but defines it just once: "I am defining hegemonic Holocaust education as projects that are sponsored by the Israeli government, and/or mainstream Jewish organizations." Since Peto thinks (mistakenly) that "hegemonic" is a pejorative term, she defines it as whatever Israel or Jews do.

What distinguished Peto's rehashing of the ravings of the *Protocols of the Elders of Zion*, as modernized by assorted Chomskys, Finkelsteins, and Walt-Mearsheimers, was her dedication of the thesis to her dead and defenseless grandmother, Jolan Peto: "If she were alive today, she would be right there with me protesting against Israeli apartheid." Like most dead people, Peto's grandmother is vulnerable to assaults on her memory by an unscrupulous and ruthless grandchild. (Jewish *mothers*, one notices, rarely receive these accolades from their Israel-hating daughters; often still alive, mothers constitute too great a risk.)

But, although unlucky in her granddaughter, Jolan Peto has been redeemed by her grandson, a Houston physician named David Peto. He published on December 16, 2010 an open letter to the press in which he urged his sister to respect the dead and cease to conscript their grandmother for her sordid vendetta against the Jews:

> It is not my desire to get involved with the details of my sister Jenny Peto's thesis, which has recently generated tremendous controversy. There are people far more qualified than I to debate the merits of the thesis, or lack thereof. There is, however, one point that I would like to contest. My sister dedicated her thesis to our late grandmother, Jolan Peto. She asserted that if our grandmother "were alive today, she would be right there with me protesting against Israeli apartheid." Our grandmother was the youngest teacher at the Jewish orphanage in Budapest during the Second World War. She, along with my grandfather, saved countless children from death at the hands of the Nazis. After the war, she saw firsthand the brutality and baseness of the communist regime that came into power. She, along with our grandfather and father, escaped to Canada, and celebrated the day of their arrival each and every year. Freedom was not an abstract idea to her; it was alive and tangible for her. Our grandmother was a soft-spoken woman, but she had an iron will. She taught us to abhor hatred, and to strive for excellence in everything we did. She was a woman of endless patience and generosity, and boundless love. She was uncompromising in her dedication to truth and honesty, and was also an ardent supporter of the state of Israel. My sister is simply wrong; our grandmother would have been entirely opposed to her anti-Israel protests. Our grandmother had a tremendous impact on my life, and her memory continues to be a source of strength and inspiration to my family. My daughter is named after her, and we pray that she will emulate her namesake. I cannot in good conscience allow my sister to misappropriate publicly our grandmother's memory to suit her political ideology.

For this act of decency, Dr. Peto was pilloried by his ever-predictable sister for being "a right-wing fanatical, racist Zionist."

The other "useful idiot" (and cemetery desecrator) to whom Kay alluded is one Judy Rebick. She is a practitioner of no known discipline at all (not even the one prohibited by W. H. Auden's Eleventh Commandment: "Thou shalt not commit sociology"). Rather, she is a "chaired" professor (at Ryerson University in Toronto) of "Social Justice," that prolific generator of ferocious do-gooders. She is the author of a number of feminist tracts (including "Barack Obama is 'our sister's keeper'") and a book called *Politically Speaking* (coauthored with a writer named—by himself, one hopes—Kike Roach). She too has a dead grandmother to sacrifice at the antisemites' new altar. A year before Peto vaulted to international infamy, Rebick came to the defense of yet another prodigiously busy Canadian Jewish Israel-hater, Naomi Klein, by announcing in September 2009 that her own grandmother, who had survived a pogrom, indeed (she implied) *because* she had survived a pogrom, "would have been so proud of Naomi Klein" for exhorting the Toronto Film Festival to shun the city of Tel Aviv.

The line of succession among these anti-Zionist converters of their deceased grandmothers may, however, be traced a bit farther back than Kay's Canadians, to a public intellectual of far greater weight and prominence than either Rebick or Peto: England's Alain De Botton. Mr. De Botton is the author of several "self-help" books with titles like *How Proust Can Change Your Life*; and to his actual publishing record has recently been added a fictional string of titles invented by Howard Jacobson in *The Finkler* Question. This satirical novel portrays the spiritual anemia of England's anti-Zionist "ashamed" Jews, who are ashamed not of their own perfidy and cowardice but of Israel's existence. The character who gives the novel its name, Samuel Finkler, is a composite figure based in part on De Botton. Finkler has written such best sellers as *The Socratic Flirt* and *The Existentialist in the Kitchen*. For declaring on the BBC (just as actress Miriam Margolyes had done) that, "as a Jew," he is "ashamed" of Israel, Finkler is promptly rewarded with an invitation to join a group of "well-known theatrical and academic Jews" who offer to rename themselves, "in honour of his courage in speaking out—Ashamed Jews." Flattered by the attention of the third-rate actors, he accepts the honor. The narrator adds, for no readily apparent reason, that Finkler cares as little for the praise of his fellow academics as for "the prayers he had never said for his grandfather." The pointed acerbity of that remark about how Finkler cynically manipulates the memory of his grandfather is puzzling unless we are aware that, in this *roman à clef*, Finkler's exploitation of his grandfather is probably based upon De Botton's exploitation of *his* grandmother in the Anglo-Jewish and Israeli press.

We do not know whether De Botton—who is proud to call himself an atheist—has been more attentive to the soul of his grandmother than that of his grandfather, but, like his Canadian emulators, he has gone to the trouble of disinterring and resurrecting her, as if to invoke ancestral authority for his repudiation of his ancestors. In a September 22, 2009, interview with the London *Jewish Chronicle*, De Botton replied to a question about what Israel meant to him as follows: "Israel is for me a country I will always associate with my grandmother, Yolande Gabai, who played a central role in the founding of the state through her activities in Egypt with the Jewish Agency, a country whose current state she would deplore, for she knew that peace with the Arabs was at the core of the challenge facing the new country." We are all too familiar with the smug, self-satisfied assurance of these smelly little orthodoxies about "deplorable" Israel. They say, in effect, the following: "Despite superficial evidence to the contrary, such as the absence of peace since Israel's unilateral withdrawal from Lebanon in favor of Hizbullah and from Gaza in favor of Hamas, all of us thinking people who read the *Independent*, the *Guardian*, the *Observer*, and the *New Statesman* know that Israel is responsible for the absence of peace with its neighbors because it has not yet fully withdrawn from the disputed territories of Judea and Samaria (which, you may recall, were entirely in the hands of the Arabs, theirs to do with whatever they liked, from 1948 to 1967, when they decided to go to war against Israel)." But this is not quite blatant and gross enough for De Botton: he must also invoke the authority of his dead grandmother.

Yolande Gabai Harmor De Botton was indeed an important figure in the Zionist movement. Born in Alexandria, Egypt, she spied for the Jewish Agency during 1947–48, risking both her own life and that of her son while posing as a *Palestine Post* journalist, and earning the nickname of "the Jewish Mata Hari." In July 1948 she was imprisoned in Egypt and later deported. In 1948–49 she worked for the Middle East Department of the Israeli Foreign Ministry. She died in 1959, ten years before her grandson Alain was born, and left behind precious little evidence that she would have become a willing recruit to the view of Anglo-Jewish leftists that if Israel has a *raison d'être* at all, it is, as De Botton suggested in an egregious interview with *Ha'aretz* in October 2008, to "humiliate" Arabs and "kill" their olive trees. (Allegations of Israeli attacks on Arab olive trees flare up frequently in the propaganda war conducted by Arabs and Arabophiles in the west. Although never attaining the scale of such gigantic frauds as "Jeningrad" or "Mohammed al-Dura," they never go away either. In October 2002, for example, as a distraction from the news of the latest intifada savagery, *bien-pensant* Jewish leftists shrieked about "the cruel and vindictive destruction of . . . venerable olive groves under the pretext that they were hiding places for snipers." Alas, as Israel Radio reported, the terrorist who had just murdered two little Jewish girls and a woman in Hermesh exploited the olive trees to reconnoiter the area and then slip under the fence to do his murderous work.)

De Botton seems to take the fact that his grandmother got along nicely in Egyptian society (while concealing her work as a spy!) and believed the foundation of a Jewish state would benefit Arabs (toward whom she felt kindly) as well as Jews proves, beyond doubt, that she would now, if resurrected, be an avid conscript to his own trendy prejudices and the "Palestinian" irredentist cause. Ben-Gurion, of course, believed the very same thing that Grandma Yolande did, but he has yet to be conscripted by the grave robbers. Moreover, it does not occur to De Botton that the Palestinians have become one of the world's most ruined peoples not because Jews won't "make peace" with them but because, encouraged by the Petos, Rebicks, and De Bottons, they have devoted themselves not to the building up of their own society but to the destruction of the society of their neighbor.

In addition to being a writer (at times, as in *The Pleasures and Sorrows of Work*, a good one), De Botton is the founder of an institution in central London called "The School of Life." Repudiating the Renaissance tradition of liberal (or "useless") education in favor of what John Henry Newman (in *The Idea of a University*) called the servile (or "useful") kind, the school offers courses in (to quote De Botton) "marriage, child-rearing, choosing a career, changing the world and death." The curriculum does not, however, appear to include a course in the Fifth Commandment, and De Botton's violation of the injunction to honor your father and mother (and, by extension, your grandfather and grandmother) suggests that he (and Peto and Rebick and all the other aspiring Jewish Mormons) would do well to make honest people of themselves before setting out to convert the dead and change the world.

14

Jewish Boycotters of Israel: How the Academic Boycott Began (2003)

On April 6, 2002, 123 university academics and researchers (their number would later rise to 250) from across Europe signed an open letter, published in Britain's *Guardian* newspaper, calling for a moratorium on all cultural and research links with Israel until the Israeli government abided by (unspecified) UN resolutions and returned yet again to negotiations with Yasser Arafat to be conducted in accordance with the principles laid down in the latest Saudi peace plan. The petition was organized and published at the very time Israelis were being butchered on a daily basis, mainly by brainwashed teenage suicide bombers, Arab versions of the Hitler Youth. It declared, in high Pecksniffian style, that since the Israeli government was "impervious to moral appeals from world leaders," Israel's cultural and research institutions should be denied further funding from the European Union and the European Science Foundation. It neglected to recommend that the European Union suspend its very generous financing of Yasser Arafat or that Chinese scholars be boycotted until China withdraws from Tibet. The petition was the brainchild of Steven Rose, the Jewish director of the Brain and Behavior Research Group at Gresham College, London, and the great majority of its signatories were British. But it included academics from a host of European countries, a number sufficient to give it the appearance of a pan-European campaign against the Jews. It had the obligatory display Israeli, one Eva Jablonka of Tel Aviv University. Nine other Israeli leftists added their names as soon as they found out about the project.

In June, Mona Baker, director of the Center for Translation and Intercultural Studies at the University of Manchester Institute of Science and Technology (UMIST) decided to practice what the all-European petitioners had preached: she dismissed from the boards of the two journals she owns and edits two Israelis, Miriam Shlesinger of Bar-Ilan University and Gideon Toury of Tel Aviv University. She also added that she would no longer accept articles from Israeli researchers, and it was later revealed that she would not "allow" books originating from her private publishing house (St. Jerome) to be purchased by Israeli institutions. One paradox of the firing, which would be repeated often in later stages of the boycott, was that Shlesinger was a member in good standing of the Israeli left, former chairman of Amnesty International's Israeli chapter, and ever at the ready with "criticism of Israeli policies in the West Bank." Toury, for his part, opposed taking any retaliatory action against Baker—this had been proposed by an American teaching fellow at Leeds named Michael Weingrad—because "a boycott is a boycott is a boycott." A small contingent of Toury's (mostly British) friends in linguistics issued a statement objecting to his dismissal because: "We agree with Noam Chomsky's view that one does not boycott people or their cultural institutions as an expression of political protest."

It was hard to say whether this document was more notable for its lack of Jewish self-respect or for sheer ignorance (of the fact that Chomsky was leading the American campaign for disinvestment in Israel, the economic phalanx of the professorial campaign to demonize and isolate Israel). A few (non-British) members of Baker's boards resigned because they objected to the dismissal of people solely "on the basis of [their] passport," especially by a journal entitled *The Translator: Studies in Intercultural Communication*. But, for the most part, the dismissals raised no public opposition from within the British university system, just as almost none had been raised back in April when the racist hoodlum Tom Paulin, stalwart of the IRA school of poetics and lecturer at Oxford, had urged that American Jews living in the disputed territories of Judea and Samaria "should be shot dead."

The situation changed only when a prominent American scholar, Professor Stephen Greenblatt of Harvard, intervened. After arriving in England in early July 2002 to receive an honorary degree from London University, Greenblatt called Baker's actions "repellent," "dangerous," and "intellectually and morally bankrupt." "Excluding scholars because of the passports that they carry or because of their skin color, religion or political party, corrupts the integrity of intellectual work," he added.

Greenblatt's statement forced the British public to pay attention to Baker's boycott. Even a writer for the venomously anti-Israel *Guardian* was emboldened to criticize the way in which the European boycotters' petition was being carried to extreme and radical form in Britain: a British lecturer working at Tel Aviv University applied for a post back home in the United Kingdom and was told by the head of the first department to which he applied, "No, we don't accept any applicants from a Nazi state."

Greenblatt was still treating the boycott mainly as a violation of academic freedom—plausibly enough, since Rose had declared that "Academic freedom I find a completely spurious argument." But the real issue was an antisemitic campaign to transform the pariah people into the pariah state, as became evident in the rhetorically violent reactions to Greenblatt's criticism. Baker herself quickly announced that she repented of nothing. She was "not against Israeli nationals per se; only Israeli institutions as part of the Israeli state which I absolutely deplore." She was acting on behalf of good Europeans everywhere, and refused to reveal where she herself was born—Egypt, as it happens.

Greenblatt was also assaulted by another inhabitant of the academic fever swamps of Manchester, Baker's colleague Michael Sinnott, a professor of "paper science." Springing chivalrously to Baker's defense, he called Greenblatt's open letter to her "sanctimonious claptrap," decried Israel as "the mirror-image of Nazism," and asserted that what made Israel a unique menace to the world was "the breathtaking power of the American Jewish lobby." In a seven-year sojourn at the University of Illinois in Chicago, he had felt the power of the insatiable Jews on his own pulses. First, "the Israeli atrocities for which my tax dollars were paying were never reported in the American news media, which were either controlled by Jews, or browbeaten by them in the way you have just exemplified"; second, his "pay raises at UIC never really recovered" from his defiantly scheduling a graduate class on the Jewish Sabbath. The UMIST administration, already busy distancing itself from Baker, now had a still greater embarrassment on its hands when the *Sunday Telegraph* (September 29) reported Sinnott's letter. It "launched an investigation" into the abstruse question of whether Sinnott might be an antisemite. Sinnott, ever mindful of his "pay raises," issued a weasely statement of regret, not over his sin but over its detection.

As the boycott campaign intensified, its guiding lights were plagued by problems of definition bearing a ghoulish resemblance to those that once beset the Nazis in deciding just which people were to be considered fitting victims of discrimination, oppression, and (eventually) murder. Perhaps this is why Baker struck up an acquaintance with David Irving, who in December reported on his web site that she had kindly taken the trouble to alert him to an ad placed by Amazon.com in the Israeli press that might be considered supportive of that terrible country. The Hitler-loving historian could have supplied Baker with information about problems the Nazis faced in implementing their boycott: Should the targeted group be people with four Jewish grandparents or perhaps just two? Some Baker defenders had chastised Greenblatt for suggesting that it was their Israeli nationality that led to the sacking of the two Israelis. By no means! It was just the fact that they worked for Israeli universities. But what of Arabs who worked for Israeli universities? If the Hebrew University employee whose mass murder of the people in the Mount Scopus Campus cafeteria was the perfect existential realization of the boycotters' ideas had survived his exploit, would he have been banned from joining Baker's janitorial staff in Manchester?

There was also the problem of ideology. Could the professors who organized the boycott have been so ignorant of the Israeli political scene as not to know that the Israeli professoriat is the center of anti-Zionist polemic and political activity in the country? Many of the targets of the boycott would inevitably be people with political views similar to those of the boycotters themselves, especially the assumption that it is "occupation" that leads to Arab hatred of Israel, and not Arab hatred of Israel that leads to occupation.

The most paradoxical example of the boycott's effect was Israeli Oren Yiftachel, a political geographer from Ben-Gurion University, described by *Ha'aretz* as "hold[ing] extreme leftist political views." Yiftachel had coauthored a paper with an Arab Israeli political scientist from Haifa University named As'ad Ghanem, dealing with the attitude of Israeli authorities to Arabs within Israel proper and the disputed territories. They submitted it to the English periodical *Political Geography*, whose editor, David Slater, returned it with a note saying it had been rejected because its authors were Israelis.

Here was a case to test the mettle of a boycotter! A *mischling* article, half-Jewish, half-Arab, wholly the product of people carrying Israeli passports and working for Israeli institutions, yet expressing opinions on Israel as the devil's laboratory indistinguishable from Slater's. Poor Slater, apparently unable to amputate the Jewish part of the article from the Arab part and (to quote him) "not sure to what extent [the authors] had been critical of Israel," rejected the submission in its entirety. Or so it seemed—for after half a year of wrangling, it emerged that Slater might accept the paper if only its authors would insert some more paragraphs likening Israel to apartheid South Africa. In other words, the Englishman might relax his boycotting principles if his ideological prejudices could be satisfied.

Exactly what happened at this point is not easy to discover. Since Yiftachel is one of those Israeli academics who adheres to the motto "the other country, right or wrong," it is hard to believe he would balk at describing Israel as an apartheid state. He had in the past denounced Israeli governments as racist or dictatorial and had coauthored with Ghanem a piece in *Ha'aretz* urging Jews to participate in the Arabs' "Land Day." But now he had become the classic instance of somebody "hoist with his own petard," caught in his own trap. At one point he complained to Slater "that rejecting a person because of his [national] origin, from an academic point of view, is very problematic." Not only did it interfere with the progress of Yiftachel's career; it hurt the anti-Israel cause. "From a political and practical point of view, the boycott actually weakens the sources of opposition to the Israeli occupation in universities," he fretted. Unlucky Yiftachel found that when he and his colleague carried their message about Israeli wickedness to America, audiences would constantly pester them about—the boycott. Nor was this the only instance in which the boycott threatened to backfire. Susan Greenfield, neurobiologist and director of the Royal Institution, England's oldest independent research body, published a warning on December 14 that the boycott, "if it continues . . . will harm people in every sphere, but in medical research lives are potentially at risk."

In 1941 Otto Warburg, one of Germany's preeminent cancer researchers, was facing dismissal from his post at the Kaiser Wilhelm Society because of his "half-Jewish" origins. Hitler, aware of the value of Warburg's research to the health of German citizens, alerted Goering, who promptly turned Warburg into a "quarter Jew." Would the new boycotters emulate the (occasional) pragmatism of their predecessors, or stick firmly to their principles in order to reduce Israel to pariah status? More importantly, will the European Union, many of whose prominent members either participated or acquiesced in the destruction of European Jewry in the years 1933–45, put a stop to the conspiracy of these spiritual descendants of those Max Weinreich famously called "Hitler's professors" to expel the Jews (once again) from the family of nations? The question remains open.

15

America's Academic Boycotters: The Enemies of Israel Neither Slumber nor Sleep (2013)

"Have we indeed sinned more than any other nation?"
—Chaim Kaplan, *The Warsaw Diary* (September 10, 1939)

"In the modern world, the Jew has perpetually been on trial; still today the Jew is on trial, in the person of the Israeli—and this modern trial of the Jew, this trial which never ends, begins with the trial of Shylock."
—Philip Roth, *Operation Shylock* (1993)

If there are still many Americans who believe that college and university professors are harmless drudges obsessed with moldy futilities, people who know so much about so little that they can neither be contradicted nor are worth contradicting, they should be disabused of their illusions by the recent decisions of three (ostensibly) academic organizations to boycott the academic institutions of the state of Israel. First came the Asian American Studies Association in April 2013, and more recently the American Studies Association and the Council of Native Americans and Indigenous Studies Association. All have decided that they can no longer share the globe with a Jewish-majority state, any more than the academics included in Max Weinreich's classic study of *Hitler's Professors* (YIVO, 1946) could continue to share Europe with its Jewish minority. It was these German professors who made antisemitism academically respectable and complicit in raw murder. They called into question—and quite successfully, of course—the Jews' "right to live"; our homegrown antisemites—and let us not flinch from calling them what they are—now dispute Israel's "right to exist," making themselves accessories before the fact to the planned erasure of Israel by Iran and its Arab satellites. When the new, academic version of the 1933 Nazi boycotts began, ten years ago in England, it appealed to Europeans who were convinced that the Holocaust had given antisemitism a bad name, and that it deserved another chance. Now it has found a foothold in America's universities.

The politicization of professional organizations, especially in the humanities, has a long history in this country. Those among us who have passed our biblical threescore and ten were reminded by the Americanists' decision to read Israel out of the family of nations of one Louis Kampf, who in 1971 was installed as president of the Modern Language Association (MLA) for the express purpose of imposing the values of the New Left. He was to supply teachers who never cared much for literature in the first place a rationale for their hostility to literary studies: the great literary works were nothing but an instrument and a result of class oppression. Kampf and his acolytes, instead of applying for job retraining, envisioned revolution via the English departments. Overcome by the explosive power of boredom, they would "liberate" campus buildings in which they could make literature "relevant." (I still recall a late colleague of mine who, when asked at the time why she had not renewed her MLA membership, replied, "As a Canadian citizen, I'm not permitted to join foreign political organizations.")

The New Left, despite (or because) of its heavily Jewish contingent, seething with yet unabated hatred of Israel for surviving the Six-Day War, in later years (1998) would also elect Edward Said, the "professor of terror" and veteran of the PLO executive, to the presidency of the MLA. Cynthia Ozick had remarked of Said's joining of literature to terror that "if, years ago when I was in graduate school, someone had told me that it was possible to be steeped in Joseph Conrad and at the same time be a member of the 'National Council' of a world-wide terror organization I would have doubted this with all the passion for civilization and humane letters that a naïve and literature-besotted young person can evidence. I know better now. Professor Said has read *Heart of Darkness*, and it has not educated his heart."[1]

In January of 2014 the same MLA, an organization whose 30,000 members dwarf the membership of the American Studies Association, will devote a panel of its annual meeting to a "debate" of the boycott, perhaps the prelude to a resolution proposing an MLA variant. One of the proboycott panelists is Barbara Harlow of the University of Texas, who has been a busy virtuoso of anti-Israel activity since at least 1989, when she sprang to the defense of Said for having insisted on the "right" of the PLO, supposedly guaranteed by the UN Charter itself, "to punish collaborators during periods of military occupation." The other four MLA panelists, in a remarkable display of what progressives mean by "diversity," also favor the BDS movement, though not all have any connection with literature or philology, the ostensible business of the MLA.

Many of Said's disciples would go on to concoct a heady brew of postmodernist theorizing, infatuation with terror against Israel and America, and stupefyingly opaque prose. Here, for example, is Gayatri Chakravorty Spivak, as heavily petted by Columbia University today as Said was years ago by that noble institution, in a lecture of 2002: "Suicide bombing—and the planes of 9/11 were living bombs—is a purposive self-annihilation, a confrontation between oneself and oneself, the extreme end of auto-eroticism, killing oneself as other, in the process killing others. . . .Suicidal resistance is a message inscribed on the body when no other means will get through. It is both execution and mourning . . . you die with me for the same cause, no matter which side you are on. Because no matter who you are there are no designated killees [sic] in suicide bombing. . . . It is a response . . . to the state terrorism practiced outside of its own ambit by the United States and in the Palestinian case additionally to an absolute failure of hospitality."[2] On such ingredients, which Lionel Trilling used to call "the language of nonthought," does our professorial avant-garde nourish itself.

The allegations against Israel brought by the assorted academic boycotters are countless, and make the tiny country—that "shitty little country," as a French diplomat who unzipped his mouth in public said a few years ago—guilty of virtually every evil on the planet with the (possible) exception of global warming. But let us examine the favorite one: Israel is an "apartheid" state. According to the U.S. Campaign for the Academic and Cultural Boycott of Israel, "All academic exchanges with Israeli academics . . . have the effect of normalizing Israel and its politics of occupation and apartheid." On every American campus that deems itself "progressive," there is an Israel Apartheid Week every spring. For days on end the self-declared friends of the human species spew fire and vitriol at the Jewish state and call for its elimination from the family of nations, so that the globe may be *Judenstaatrein* (purified of a Jewish state).

There have never been apartheid laws in Israel. Jews and Arabs use the same buses, clinics, government offices, universities, theaters, restaurants, soccer fields, and beaches. All citizens of Israel, regardless of religion or ethnic origin, are equal before the law. That law accords full political, civil, and human rights to all its people, including the more than one million Arab citizens, some of whom serve in the Israeli parliament and cabinet. Israel is also the only country in the world to have sought out and brought to its shores, entirely on its own initiative, tens of thousands of black Africans for purposes other than slavery, granting them full citizenship. There is, to be sure, extreme and murderous racial and religious discrimination in the Middle East—have the Americanists looked into the causes of the 130,000 dead in nearby Syria?—so much so that Israel is nearly the only state in the region where "apartheid" is *not* practiced in some form.

Anybody who believes that the singling out of Israel, the sole Jewish-majority nation among all the nations of the world, for boycott has nothing to do with Jew-hatred will also believe that Europe's recent obsession with banning circumcision and the laws of kashrut has nothing to do with a deep-seated desire to rid itself, yet again, of Jews. Such a (conjectural) person might also be interested in some choice real estate I know about in downtown Aleppo.

The American Studies Association boycotters, especially the organization's president and executive committee, have comported themselves with the dogmatism and dictatorialness that have long been *de rigueur* among academic liberals: they would not allow their opponents within the ASA to make the case against declaring war on Israel to the organization's membership. They also acted according to rule in trotting out their Display Jews (to borrow Kafka's term) to blacken Israel's image (and turn the pariah people into the pariah state). This stale trick is the ASA's chief defense against charges that the boycott movement is antisemitic. One hesitates to call such Jews self-haters because so many of them are sick with self-love. Seen in long historical perspective, they represent a relatively recent development in the often desperate search for Jewish "identity." They become Jews by virtue of the (much-advertised) fact that they are *not* Zionists. These Jews inspire contempt but also—let me confess it—a certain degree of pity. The creation of the state of Israel just a few years after the destruction of European Jewry was one of the greatest affirmations by a martyred people of the will to live, indeed one of the most hopeful signs for humanity since the dove brought to Noah "an olive leaf freshly plucked" after the primeval flood had abated. What, I wonder, must it be like for a Jew to be blind to this?

Perhaps a cautionary and charitable note of warning to the aforementioned "non-Zionist Jews" assiduously feeding the flames of antisemitism is in order. Stoking this fire is a risky business because the flames quickly get out of control. Jew-haters, whether Nazi or Communist, Islamist or progressive, are notoriously poor at distinguishing between Zionist and anti-Zionist Jews. Like poor Cinna, the unfortunate poet in *Julius Caesar* who is mistaken by the "firebrands" come to mourn their murdered emperor, and who insists that he is *not* "Cinna the conspirator," it will avail them nothing to plead, "I am Professor Dryasdust the anti-Zionist! I am not Melamed Dryasdust the Zionist." The mob will nevertheless reply, "It is no matter. Tear him to pieces, he's a Jew."[3]

Jews who eagerly look forward to the elimination of Israel by relentless demonization and its likely sequel, by fair means or foul, might do well to remember the old Yiddish proverb: *Come for your inheritance, and you may have to pay for the funeral.*

Notes

1. *New Leader*, August 11, 1980.
2. Michael Weingrad's transcription of this lecture appeared in the July 29, 2002, online edition of the *New Republic*: http://tnr.com/doc.mhtml?i=20020729& s=notebook072902bush.
3. See Cynthia Ozick on Judith Butler in "The Modern 'Hep! Hep! Hep!'" in *The Jewish Divide over Israel*, ed. Edward Alexander and Paul Bogdanor (New Brunswick, NJ: Transaction, 2006), 5–6.

16

Jews against Themselves: The BDS Movement and Modern Apostasy (2014)

"The spiritual father of the fanatical incitement against the Jews was Abner of Burgos, a Jewish kabbalist and scholar who converted to Christianity in about 1321, upon experiencing a deep religious and spiritual crisis, and became known as Alfonso of Valladolid. His . . . despair of the Jewish question found expression in his polemics—some written in Hebrew, others in Spanish—which contain a complete doctrine of denunciation of the Jews and their laws and morals. Oral Law, he maintained, constituted a code of robbery, usury and deception. . . . Various sayings by the Talmudic sages . . . were interpreted by this apostate to mean that the Jews must be deprived of the easy livelihoods of usury and medicine, that they must be deprived of their autonomy and that they must be terrorized and subjected to harsh laws. Only then would they merit redemption."

—H. H. Ben-Sasson, *A History of the Jewish People*

1. Prelude: At Vassar College

Starting in late February the campus of Vassar College in Poughkeepsie has been the scene of some of the ugliest depredations yet organized by the BDS (Boycott, Divestment and Sanctions) campaign designed to expel Israel from the family of nations. The college founded in the nineteenth century by a brewer has become a witches' brew of bullying and violence carried out by Students for Justice in Palestine and its collaborators. They described themselves as "staging an *action* [italics mine]" (on March 3) against the on-campus part of an international studies class that was to include a trip to the Middle East to consider "water issues" in the region. Since the Jew and then the Israeli have been perpetually on trial, it was considered necessary by Vassar to convene a special forum to consider the "ethics" of a course that would include setting foot in Israel. Although the trip's itinerary confirmed that its (predictably tendentious) purpose was to convince students that Israel is unfairly depriving Palestinian Arabs of water, that slander was not sufficient to protect it (or its garden-variety Jewish leftist instructors) from the wrath of BDSers, who consider Israel the devil's own experiment station or, in the colorful lingo of Philip Weiss, a Jewish hater of Israel in attendance at the forum, "a blot on civilization." Their violence (which included screaming, interruptions, and perhaps ululating) was the existential realization of a letter published on March 1 by a group of thirty-nine Vassar faculty members who condemned the Vassar administration for daring to criticize the recently passed resolution of the American Studies Association in favor of boycotting Israeli academic institutions.

The professors charged that critics of the ASA boycotters had had "a chilling effect on the free exchange of ideas and opinions." It is now almost sixty-five years since Lionel Trilling remarked on the way in which modern liberals not only want the right to go their own way in all things, but to go their own way without any questions ever being asked of them. Those who carried out the "action" also had their special complaint. According to Weiss they were "people of color" (perhaps by analogy with "jeans of blue"), and therefore entitled to accuse their critics of "racism." (They understand liberal left quackery only too well: liberals think "the poor" are their equals in every sense . . . except that of being equal to them.) But the final word on that allegation of "chilled" discourse was left to the gloating Weiss: "The spirit of that young progressive space was that Israel is a blot on civilization, and boycott is right and necessary. If a student had gotten up and said, I love Israel, he or she would have been mocked and scorned into silence."

Matthew Arnold, recalling (back in 1883) the happier moments of his second visit to America, expressed pleasure that "in colleges like Vassar College in the State of New York," women ("the fair host of the Amazons") were now studying Greek art and Greek literature. One wonders what he would think if he visited the same place now. I believe that what would most shock him would be not the bullying, the intimidation, the thuggery—to Oxford itself he had applied Byron's aspersion: "There are our young barbarians all at play!"—but the flagrant violation of conscience in intellectual work, a violation like the following course description by Vassar's Professor Joshua Schreier:

> History 214: The Roots of the Palestine-Israel Conflict:
> This course is NOT designed to present "an objective" account of a "two-sided" conflict. The fact that there are supposedly two sides does not obligate us to portray each as equally right and/or equally wrong. The goal, rather, is to understand why the conflict arose, and what sorts of power inequalities have made it continue.... Why and how did economic globalization, technological development, and European imperialism foster the creation of two different national identities in Palestine? Why and how and when did these two identities develop in such a way as to preclude members of certain religious or ethnic groups from belonging?

Ruth Wisse has pointed out (*Commentary*, March 2009) the impossibility of finding a course description at any elite American college or university that operated from the *opposed* ideological premise to Schreier's: namely, that "the Jewish people had a connection to the land between the Jordan River and the Mediterranean that was greater and of longer duration than the nomadic peoples who came to be called Palestinians, and that the central place of Palestinians in world politics is due to an imbalance of power between the small Jewish state and the petroleum-drenched Arab states with which it must contend."

When he wrote this description, which apparently raised no eyebrows in whatever Vassar administrators pass judgment on curriculum, Schreier was an untenured toiler in the college's Jewish Studies Program; now he is its chairman—and also (a fact that may surprise some people) the chief campus spokesman for the academic boycott of Israel. Here is how Lucette Lagnado (a Vassar graduate) reported the revelation in the *Wall Street Journal* (February 24, 2014): "The head of the Jewish Studies Program ... had also expressed support for the boycott movement. Prof. Schreier was quoted in the campus paper ruminating that while once 'instinctively against' the boycott, he had heard more 'substantiated, detailed' arguments in its behalf, and as a result 'I am currently leaning in favor of it,' he concluded delicately, as if choosing a favorite tea."

2. Self-Hatred—Or Self-Love and Apostasy?

In his formidable book entitled *Jewish Self-Hatred* (1986), Sander Gilman showed how apostasy in the form of conversion to Christianity was the solution to their personal predicament chosen by substantial numbers of disaffected European Jewish intellectuals. He concluded the book by suggesting that "one of the most recent forms of Jewish self-hatred is the virulent Jewish opposition to the existence of the State of Israel." In the modern world, however, the contradiction between liberal pieties and the defense of Israel is rarely resolved by formal apostasy, and it is difficult to find any self-hatred in such Jewish Israel-haters as Noam Chomsky, Richard Falk, Judith Butler, and Jacqueline Rose, who suffer rather from a self-love that would shame Shakespeare's Malvolio. They do on occasion cling to the outer trappings of medieval apostasy. Marc Ellis, the wandering "liberation theologian" and former director of the Center for Jewish Studies at Baylor University, famously spent one Yom Kippur publicly confessing the sins of (other) Jews against Palestinian Arabs in front of a Christian audience at the (Protestant) Union Theological Seminary. (He also praised the "courage" of Gillian Rose, sister of the aforementioned Jacqueline, for her deathbed conversion to Christianity via the Church of England.) Daniel Boyarin, the University of California, Berkeley professor (of Talmud) who has identified himself as a Jew "destined by fate, psychology, personal history, or whatever, to be drawn to Christianity," warns that "my Judaism may be dying at Nablus, Daheishe, Beteen" (i.e., places the Israeli army has entered to pursue people inclined to massacre Jews). Noam Chomsky favors St. Paul's Cathedral, in (or in front of) which he has often held forth, in one instance introduced by another perfervid Jewish Israelophobe, the late Harold Pinter, who introduced Chomsky as "the leading critical voice against the criminal regime now running the United States." (Lest that remark prove overly cryptic, the ever-helpful Chomsky had a few weeks earlier clarified: "Antisemitism is no longer a problem [in the U.S.], fortunately. It's raised, but it's raised because privileged people want to make sure they have total control, not just 98% control."

These, however, are but the dramaturgy, the trappings and suits of woe where "virulent Jewish opposition to the existence of the state of Israel" is concerned. We see it more frequently, and frighteningly, in the BDS movement, dedicated to turning the pariah people into the pariah nation by calling into question Israel's "right to exist," just as the Nazis had called into question, and very successfully, the Jewish people's "right to live." The leaders of this movement are preponderantly Jewish apostates of a new kind that may well frighten us. Cynthia Ozick explains:

> The Nicholas Donins and Pablo Christianis of ages past ran to abandon their Jewish ties even as they subverted them. The Nicholas

Donins and Pablo Christianis of our own time run to embrace their Jewish ties even as they besmirch them. So it is as self-declared Jews, as loyal and honorable Jews, as Jews in the line of the prophets, as Jews who speak out for the sake of the integrity of Jews and Judaism, that we nowadays hear arguments against the survival, or the necessity, or the legitimacy, of the State of Israel.

3. The Jews of BDS

Despite its precedents in the Nazis' *kauf nicht bei Juden* campaign begun in 1933 and the expulsion of Jews from German universities by "Hitler's professors," and the Arab economic boycott of Israel now over sixty-five years old, the BDS movement, especially its leadership, may fairly be called, despite local variations, "Jews against Themselves." It was begun in England in April 2002 by the Jewish academic Steven Rose and his wife, Hilary. Espousal of the boycott of Israel, especially its academic institutions, soon became the identifying mark of "progressive" English Jews, so much so that Howard Jacobson devoted a whole satirical novel (*The Finkler Question*, 2010) to "the Jews of shame," people who were ashamed of Israel's very existence, though not of their own illiteracy, cowardice, and treachery.

Sixty years earlier it was a widespread joke that "when a man can no longer be a Jew, he becomes a Zionist." But in *The Finkler Question* characters are far more likely to believe, as one named Kugel explicitly states: "I am a Jew because I am a non-Zionist." Another character, almost certainly based on the actor Stephen Fry, is described as follows: "To be an ASHamed Jew did not require that you had been knowingly Jewish all your life. Indeed, one among them only found out he was Jewish at all in the course of making a television programme in which he was confronted on camera with *who he really was*. In the final frame of the film he was disclosed weeping before a memorial in Auschwitz to dead ancestors who until that moment he had never known he'd had. . . . Born a Jew on Monday, he had signed up to be an ASHamed Jew by Wednesday and was seen chanting 'We are all Hezbollah' outside the Israeli Embassy on the following Saturday."

Another Anglo-Jewish tribune of the BDS movement, and not merely a fictional one, is the very ashamed Jacqueline Rose, the psychoanalytically inclined professor of English. In the nosology of social diseases she merits a special place. She has long been so consumed by shame that she insists only the erasure of Israel can cure her affliction: "Appalled at what the Israeli nation perpetrated in my name," she has repeatedly expressed the wish to live "in a world in which we did not have to be ashamed of shame" and looks forward to curing her shame-sickness by destroying its cause: Israel.

In America the most flagrant, blatant, and obscene Jewish defamer of Israel has been a figure with global reach through a megaphone of Brobdingnagian proportions. Richard Falk recently completed a six-year term as a United Nations "rappporteur" (literally "talebearer") for human rights in the "Palestinian territories"—this after forty years as professor of international studies at Princeton University. He had also acquired fame outside of academia as a regular in the *New York Review of Books* (the *Women's Wear Daily* of anti-Israel Jews), and once again in 1989 when, in a *Commentary* dispute (with me) over Edward Said's claim that the UN charter entitled the PLO to murder "collaborators," he praised Said as "this courageous and compassionate person who [sic] many of us value." From his UN post Falk has relentlessly described Israel as Satan's lair, called for "a legitimacy war against Israel," blamed the Boston Marathon bombings on "Tel Aviv," and then—in the summer of 2011—having exhausted his own store of verbal eloquence on the topic, posted on his "blog" site a cartoon of a dog wearing a yarmulke urinating on a blindfolded female figure of Justice. If any single figure ever embodied the image of the UN as the center of the world's evil, it is Richard Falk. But—it is almost needless to add—this did not stop him from placing himself in the line of Jewish biblical prophets working for "social justice" by leading the international assault on Israel for countless human rights violations.

Second only to Falk as the public face of the BDS movement to blacken Israel's reputation and caricature Zionism is Judith Butler, a professor of philosophy with a mind so coarse that it sees in the establishment of Israel not one of the few redeeming events in a century of blood and shame, not one of the noblest examples of a commitment to life by a martyred people, not an expression of the yearning for human dignity symbolized by the Exodus from slavery that has characterized Jewish civilization for millennia, but an emotional quirk, a stupid prejudice, no more worthy of respect or preservation than a taste for high-cholesterol foods. "Some Jews have a heartfelt investment in corned beef sandwiches," she sneers. So what?

Butler is a latter-day descendant of what has been called the California School of Jewish Studies, to which she arrived after establishing herself as a theoretician of "queer theory" as well as a member of that cadre of philosophy and literature teachers who hate both for being at once the instruments and results of class and gender oppression. Like the aforementioned Boyarin, who sought to make the "feminized Jewish man" into a universal model, she belongs to the Queer Nation, and believes that sexual identity is arbitrarily constructed independently of biology. Not for her the old wisecrack about how "language has gender, people have sex." But what has remained most constant in her movement from philosophy to anti-Zionist politics is the stupefying opacity of her prose, as epitomized in the following (award-winning) sentence.

> The move from a structuralist account in which capital is understood to structure social relations in relatively homologous ways to a view of hegemony in which power relations are subject to repetition, convergence, and rearticulation brought the question of temporality into the thinking of structure, and marked a shift from a form of Althusserian theory that takes structural totalities as theoretical objects to one in which the insights into the contingent possibility of structure inaugurate a renewed conception of hegemony as bound up with the contingent sites and strategies of the rearticulation of power.

This from the winner of the Theodor Adorno Prize, chaired professor of rhetoric and comparative literature at Berkeley, occupant of the Hannah Arendt chair in the European Graduate School in Switzerland, recipient of numerous honorary degrees. Among the many awards lavished upon Butler this is surely the most deserved. The sentence appeared in the journal *Diacritics* in 1997 and won the annual Bad Writing Contest conducted by the journal *Philosophy and Literature*.

Prior to autumn 2003 Butler was someone who defined her "Jewishness" in opposition to the state of Israel. She was mainly a signer of petitions harshly critical of the state. She did express misgiving about signing *one* petition (for halting American aid) because it "was not nearly strong enough . . . it did not call for the end of Zionism." Upon looking more deeply into the matter, she discovered that there had been "debates among Jews throughout the 19th and early 20th centuries as to whether Zionism ought to become the basis of a state." From this she swiftly concluded that demanding an end to Zionism in 2003, calling for politicide, was no different from taking a debater's position against it fifty years before the state came into existence.

The *annus mirabilis* of what has become her life struggle against Zion began in September 2002 when Lawrence Summers, then president of Harvard, delivered a speech deploring the upsurge of antisemitism in many parts of the globe: he included synagogue bombings, physical assaults on Jews, desecration of Jewish holy places, and (this with special emphasis) denial of the right of "the Jewish state to exist." But his most immediate concern was that "at Harvard and . . . universities across the country" faculty-initiated petitions were calling "for the University to single out Israel among all nations as the lone country where it is inappropriate for any part of the university's endowment to be invested." (Summers's speech stands to this day as a rare exception to the timidity of university administrators in facing up to the true nature of BDS activities, and it may have contributed to his being forced out of Harvard's presidency in February 2006, ostensibly because he had alluded to, without condemning, the view that women have less natural aptitude for science than men.)

Butler had herself signed the same petition in Berkeley, where it circulated in February 2001. She therefore found Summers's remarks not only wrong but personally "hurtful" since they implicated Butler herself in the newly resurgent campus antisemitism as well as the violence it quickly fomented. (She could hardly have failed to notice that the Berkeley BDS petition provided the impetus for anti-Israel mob violence at her own campus on April 24, 2001, a few weeks after it had been circulated, and for more explicitly anti-*Jewish* mobs at nearby San Francisco State University in May of the following year.) She therefore decided to write a reply to Summers in the *London Review of Books*, whose main political impulse is the unwillingness to share the globe with a Jewish majority state. Her essay, entitled "No, It Isn't Anti-Semitic," published August 21, 2003, is a key document of the BDS movement and as central to "antisemitism denial" as the work of Robert Faurisson is to Holocaust denial. It operates, moreover, at the same intellectual level as the Frenchman's work.

Summers, knowing how ubiquitous in anti-Israel discourse is the straw man called "the defender of Israel who decries any criticism of Israeli policy as antisemitism," had gone out of his way to separate himself from this (entirely conjectural) figure, but to no avail. Butler has continued, with steam engine regularity, to insist that it is "untrue, absurd and painful for anyone to argue that those who formulate a criticism of the State of Israel is [sic] antisemitic or, if Jewish, self-hating." She further accused Summers of striking a blow against academic freedom because his words were having "a chilling effect on academic discourse." (Do Butler's words sound familiar? That is because she had performed—"performativity" is her academic hobbyhorse—at Vassar not long before the aforementioned thirty-nine professors complained that criticisms of the American Studies Association had nearly frozen *their* vocal chords.) No evidence is (or indeed could be) adduced for Butler's allegation. Of one thing we can be sure: the chill did not take hold at Harvard itself, which would very soon (in November) play host to Oxford's Tom Paulin, who had urged (in yet another "criticism of Israeli policy") that Jews living in Judea/Samaria "should be shot dead," or at Columbia, where Paulin continued merrily through autumn semester as a visiting professor, or at the *New York Review of Books*, which in October 2003 would publish Tony Judt's call for an end to the state of Israel, or in the *London Review of Books itself*, which in January 2003 published another 133 lines of Paulin doggerel called "On Being Dealt the Anti-Semitic Card," a versified regurgitation of Butler's "No, It's Not Anti-Semitic." If Summers's Harvard speech had a chilling effect on antisemitic clarion calls, including incitement to raw murder, one would not wish to know what the fully heated versions sound like.

Although Butler's assault on Summers is a loose, baggy monster, what it leaves out is more blatant than what it includes. Like all BDS manifestos, it omits history altogether, distorts evidence, and omits context. Did it never occur to Butler that the divestment campaign is one prong of the endless Arab campaign to strangle the Jewish state? The "occupation" that Butler and fellow BDSers constantly bemoan did not cause Arab hatred and violence; it was Arab hatred and aggression that led to occupation. For nineteen years, from 1948 to 1967, the Arabs were entirely in control of the disputed territories, theirs to do with whatever they pleased; and somehow it never occurred to them to establish a state there, or indeed to use those territories as anything except staging grounds for attacks on Israel. (Are there still people outside of the State Department who believe the Arabs are as interested in having a state as in pulling down that of their neighbor?)

The Harvard/MIT divestment petition that Butler championed against Summers was promoted at MIT by Chomsky, who would be rendered nearly speechless without calling Israelis Nazis. Butler was herself one of the "first signatories" of a July 28, 2003, petition that uses the Israeli-Nazi equation (beloved of denigrators of Zionism going back to British official circles in Cairo in 1941): it says Israeli use of concrete, barbed wire, and electronic fortifications has made "Israeli citizens themselves into a people of camp wardens." So it would seem that, for Butler and her loyal followers in the BDS movement, "language plays an important role in shaping and attuning our . . . understanding of social and political realities" except when

137

it happens to be the antisemitic language that demonizes Israel as being black as Gehenna and the pit of hell.

Conclusion

In his *History of the Jews in Christian Spain*, Yitzhak Baer tells us that Abner of Burgos, the apostate cited at the beginning of this essay, not only devised a plan for terrorizing and destroying the Jews that "the enemies of Israel were to carry out in its entirety in the year 1391." "The aging fanatical apostate who wrote these diatribes," Baer adds, "launched his holy war himself, not only in words but also in deed." But our new apostates need not work so hard: they can rest content with being accessories to, rather than perpetrators of, murder. The machinery for destruction of the state of Israel is already in place. It exists not only in Iran, whose leaders explicitly call for wiping Israel off the map with nuclear weapons that they are now almost certain to obtain. The neighbors of the tiny country called Israel would be delighted to see it reduced to sandy wastes, as would countless citizens of the Dark Continent (Europe, that is) who cannot forgive the Jews for the Holocaust. If many Iranians and Europeans still deny there was a first Holocaust, that is because, as the courageous German scholar Matthias Kuntzel has observed, "every denial of the Holocaust contains an appeal to repeat it." The BDSers may be obtuse, craven, morally bankrupt, but they would also have to be deaf, dumb, and blind not to recognize the link between their efforts and the murderous intentions of those who regret the Holocaust only because—for a time—it gave antisemitism a bad name.

There is yet one more calamity that has been brought closer by the reckless Jewish promoters of BDS, a calamity that one might have expected at least the Jewish studies professors among them to think about for just a moment. "In only one respect," wrote Hillel Halkin in 2007, "are things [now] worse. In the 1930's the Jews were a people that had lost a first temple and a second one; yet as frightful as their next set of losses was to be, they did not have a third temple to risk. Today, they do. And in Jewish history, three strikes and you're out."

17

Jewish Survivors and Their Progeny against Israel (2014)

The Jewish enemies of Israel, if they are sufficiently profligate in the expenditure of claptrap, often come to the aid of her defenders. Early this summer (2014) I wrote the following paragraph in the prologue to a book (entitled *Jews against Themselves*) that I was sending off to my publisher:

> I have not attempted a systematic taxonomy of all the species of Jews arrayed under the genus "enemies of Israel," a monumental task that would require an encyclopedia to include the following: Jewish progressives against Israel; Jewish queers against Israel; *Haredim* against Israel; Holocaust survivors against Israel; children of Holocaust survivors against Israel; Jewish Voice for Peace; grandchildren of Holocaust survivors against Israel; survivors of the Warsaw Ghetto against Israel; J Street; Jewish postmodernists against Israel; Jewish Berkeley professors against Israel; post-Zionists against Israel; Jewish members of MESA (Middle East Studies Association) against Israel; Jews for Boycotting Israeli Goods (JBIG, also called, seasonally, London's Jewish Christmas carolers against Israel); and so on and on, *ad infinitum, ad nauseam*. Despite this, there will always be readers who express astonishment that there *are* Jews who question the Jewish right to live as a natural right, or hate Israel and are ashamed to have a state. Surely they are as rare as singing mice or card-playing pigs? Alas, no.

I felt more or less content with that Swiftian list, yet also sensed that something was missing from it. The recent publication, first in Britain's *Guardian* on August 15, and then in the *New York Times* on August 23, of an ad accusing Israel of genocide in Gaza and calling for "full economic, cultural, and academic boycott of Israel" told me what it was. The ad was placed by "Jewish survivors and descendants of survivors" and also "friends of survivors," "friend of many survivors," "cousins of survivors," "cousins of victims of Nazis in Ukraine," "the great-niece of an uncle who shot himself," "spouse of hidden child," and "relative of victims." Where defamation of Israel is concerned, imagination cannot keep pace with the fantastic moral coarseness of the defamers.

According to the 327 (mostly unknown) signatories of this fiery, vitriolic, and obscene assault on the state of Israel as the one true inheritor of Nazism, and on Elie Wiesel (who dares to say that Jews have done enough dying), the death factories and outdoor killing centers and vast machinery of murder of the Germans and their allies were, for those who managed to survive them, schools of moral instruction and intellectual acumen. These gifts have enabled them to pass judgment on the latest Hamas-Israel conflict and come down unreservedly on the side of Hamas, the Islamist version of Nazism whose declared purpose is to destroy Israel and "to kill Jews wherever you find them."

It does not occur to the "survivors" (if that is indeed what they really are) and their progeny that persecuting governments and persecuting religions, while breeding vices in those who hold power, are well-known to breed answering vices in those who are powerless and suffering. The signatories assume that the death camps were such seminal teachers of moral scruple that their influence has been passed on, to the children, grandchildren, and great-grandchildren of survivors. I had failed to include these genetically privileged people in my list; and their numbers are vast, perhaps uncountable, among the variegated species of Jews within the genus "Jewish enemies of Israel." A grievous omission on my part, to be sure, if the offspring of survivors, even unto the thousandth generation, are genetically authorized to decide which nations may live, and which must die.

Three names among the signatories caught my attention: Daniel Boyarin, Hedy Epstein, and Anna Baltzer. The first lists himself as "great-grandson" of victims of Nazism. A University of California, Berkeley professor (of Talmud), Boyarin has identified himself as a Jew "destined by fate, psychology, personal history, or whatever, to be drawn to Christianity," and has warned that "my Judaism may be dying at Nablus, Daheishe, Beteen" (i.e., places the Israeli army has entered to pursue people inclined to massacre Jews). Boyarin belongs to what has been called the "sissy" school of contemporary Jewish thinkers. He calls himself "oddly gendered" and would replace the "muscular" Judaism of the Zionism he hates with a feminized Judaism that he claims to find in rabbinic texts. For him the moral center of Jewish history is a celebration of the renunciation of national interest, as if that were the only criterion of a just politics. He and others in the sissy school deem it praiseworthy in Jews never (or so they believe) in the past to have picked up the gun or the knife, as if a man unable to eat should be praised for his ability to fast. But when Israel is being bombed, Boyarin is less queasy about violence, and now takes the side of Hamas, which has been firing thousands of missiles at Israeli citizens for weeks on end. No matter the circumstances, Boyarin keeps repeating, with steam engine regularity, that Jews are "collectively engaged in war/wars against Muslims," and likens all Israeli self-defense to the Nazi Holocaust.

Then there is Hedy Epstein, a professional "survivor" (she left Germany as a child in 1939) and member of the pro-Hamas International Solidarity Movement. Since she believes that slavery, like the Nazi camps, also (unwittingly) provided ethical instruction and refinement to its victims, she makes a point of turning up in marches (most recently in Ferguson, Missouri) to support African-American race racketeers like Al Sharpton and Jesse Jackson, and never misses an opportunity to spew venom at Israel. She is a ninety-year-old version of the late Rachel Corrie—inveterate, "slumming" do-gooders who confuse doing good with feeling good about what they are doing.

Anna Baltzer, popping up in the "grandchildren" category of the ad, is really Anna Piller. But after becoming a full-throated and virtually full-time apologist for Hamas, an activist (like Epstein) in the International Solidarity Movement, and in the BDS movement, she decided to conceal her identity from a still living grandmother who was both a Holocaust survivor and a strong supporter of Israel. For people like Baltzer, it is not the sin but its disclosure that must be taken seriously. The very grandmother who enabled Piller-Baltzer to preface all her solemn idiocies about Israeli "apartheid" with "as a Jew" was thus afforded some protection from knowing that her granddaughter was speechifying in Presbyterian churches and similar venues on behalf of a Jew-killing organization. (Was there ever a shrewder reply to the question "Who is a Jew?" than the one given by the Hebrew novelist Yosef Haim Brenner when he said, "A Jew is someone with Jewish grandchildren"?) In the case of Piller-Baltzer (and no doubt in scores just like it), we have the epistemological paradox of a biologically-based claim to moral wisdom that is confuted by the very ancestor invoked to justify it.

141

Perhaps the last (though not infallible) word on this latest deformation of the Holocaust should be left to the late Primo Levi, whose decency and wisdom survived in but was not created by Auschwitz:

> The "saved" of the Lager were not the best, those predestined to do good; the bearers of a message. What I had seen and lived through proved the exact contrary. Preferably the worst survived, the selfish, the violent, the insensitive, the collaborators of the "grey zones", the spies. It was not a certain rule . . . but it was, nevertheless, a rule. I felt innocent, yes, but enrolled among the saved and therefore in permanent search of a justification in my own eyes and those of others. The worst survived, that is, the fittest; the best all died. (Primo Levi, *The Drowned and the Saved*)

18

Choose Your Side: The *New York Times* or Judaism (2013)

> "How long halt ye between two opinions?"
> —1 Kings 18:21

American Jewry is often said to be divided between those who judge Judaism by the principles of the *New York Times* and those who judge the *New York Times* by the principles of Judaism. The former group was elated by University of Massachusetts professor Joseph Levine's clarion call "Questioning the Jewish State" (*Times* of March 9, 2013), which advocated the erasure of Israel from the family of nations. The latter group was dismayed and nauseated, and confirmed in its view that expecting ordinary decency from "progressive" Jewish professors is like trying to warm yourself by the light of the moon. The former, composed in large part of what Gershom Scholem called "clever Jews" who fear nothing in this world (and maybe the next as well) so much as being called "reactionary," agreed with Levine's insistence that he not be labeled antisemitic just because he singled out Israel, among all the nations of the world, as deserving of dissolution. The latter thought the real question is whether Levine should be called a moral nonentity because he has made himself an accessory before the fact to the genocide dreamed of (and already inspiring murderous action) by Ahmadinejad, Hizbullah, Erdogan, Hamas, and numerous other "Islamist" eschatologists. (I've heard some ill-tempered members of this second group say that they looked forward to a *New York Times* discussion of whether Levine himself has an inalienable "right to exist.")

Those Jews who judge the *New York Times* by the standards of Judaism believe that the creation of the state of Israel was one of the few redeeming events in a century of blood and shame, one of the greatest affirmations of the will to live ever made by a martyred people, and a uniquely hopeful sign for humanity itself. They tend also to cling to Orwell's view that some ideas—like the virtue of Jewish powerlessness—are so stupid that only intellectuals can believe them.

Those who judge Judaism by the standards of the *Times* boast (as Irving Howe put it) of not having "danced in the streets when Ben-Gurion declared that the Jews, like other peoples, had a state of their own." They believe (as does a majority of today's Germans too) that Israel is the chief obstacle to world peace, a diversion from such liberal desiderata as gay marriage and unlimited access to abortion, and indeed the principal cause of most of the world's evils with the (possible) exception of global warming.

Professor Levine's polemic draws on sources both ancient and modern. It harkens back—albeit in the clumsy and verbose manner of somebody who "unpacks" rather than articulates ideas—to the earliest known ancient, non-Jewish document that mentions Israel by name. It is found on a monument from 1215 BCE (possessed by the British Museum) in which King Merneptah, the Egyptian forerunner of Chmielnicki, Hitler, Nasser, and Ahmadinejad, declares that "Israel is extinguished, its seed is no more."

Levine, to be sure, is a philosopher, and not—on the surface, at least—a political agitator and propagandist, although he identifies himself (who could have guessed?) as a man of the left. Up to a point, Levine has some respectable predecessors among fellow philosophers. In 1932, for example, Julien Benda, a French philosopher (and novelist), addressed the "European nation" as follows: "Intellectuals of all countries, you must be the ones to tell your nations that they are always in the wrong by the single fact that they are nations. . . . Plotinus blushed at having a body. You should blush at having a nation." But whereas Benda called for philosophers of *all* nations to blush, Levine believes in blushing only by Jews for the Jewish nation. Although the imperfections he imputes to Israel because it calls itself "Jewish" manifest themselves—a hundredfold—in scores of members of the United Nations, he demands the dissolution only of the Jewish nation—not the twenty-two Arab ones, or the numerous Christian ones, or the fifty-seven members of the League of Islamic Cooperation. Like all Israel dissolutionists—one-state solution advocates, no-state solution advocates, and (this from George Steiner) "final solution" advocates—he insists that Israel cannot be both Jewish and democratic. Perhaps the *Times* will soon invite him to cast his philosophic eye over a country called the United Kingdom, widely reputed to be democratic, and yet possessed of an official Protestant church, a Protestant monarch, a Protestant educational system (and all this in a once-Catholic country).

Levine has also attached himself, not unwittingly, to what Raul Hilberg called the last version of that ever-shortening sentence that expressed Europe's anti-Jewish policies over the centuries. "The missionaries of Christianity," wrote Hilberg, "had said in effect: You have no right to live among us as Jews. The secular rulers who followed had proclaimed: You have no right to live among us. The German Nazis at last decreed: you have no right to live." Levine admits to a slight uneasiness about the resemblance between his challenging Israel's "right to exist" and the Nazis' disputing the Jews' "right to live." But confidence in his own infallibility carries him quickly over this abyss, as if it were just an unfortunate coincidence of diction and phrasing. In fact, of course, it makes him complicit in what Hannah Arendt famously defined as the crime against humanity, "an attack upon human diversity as such, that is, upon a characteristic of the 'human status' without which the very words 'mankind' or 'humanity' would be devoid of meaning."

The editors of the *Times*, inflamed by the zeal of the proselytizer, consider a Jew's polemic advocating removal of Israel from the world so valuable that, just a week later, March 17, they published what might be called "applied Levine" in the form of a lavishly illustrated cover story entitled "If There Is a Third Intifada, We Want to Be the Ones Who Started It." Levine had declared the compelling need for politicide; and here was Ben Ehrenreich offering his modest proposal explaining how and by whom it could be done. Ehrenreich had qualified for this important *NYTimes* assignment four years earlier by publishing an article in the *Los Angeles Times* entitled "Zionism Is the Problem." Not only did it prevent harmonious relations between Jews and Arabs—it introduced into a region well-known for its rich ethnic and religious diversity a monolithic Jewish state, which must, by definition, be "exclusive" or else practice "ethnic cleansing." Ehrenreich's obsession with the potentiality for Jewish ethnic cleansing, Jewish religious fanaticism, and Jewish "apartheid" contrasted sharply with his entire indifference to the actuality of what the surrounding Arab and Muslim nations have already achieved, at a cost of hundreds of thousands of lives, in all those lines of endeavor. Like Levine he had set forth the compelling urgency of politicide (dissolution would be too weak a word) for the ill-conceived and uniquely evil country called Israel. Surely the Jews were not "entitled" to a homeland just because they had had a rather rough time of it during World War II (and earlier). But Ehrenreich set a standard for hyperbolic slander that not even the Massachusetts sage Levine has been able to match: Israel is *worse* than South Africa's apartheid regime because, for no apparent reason that Ehrenreich can think of, it attacks civilians in Gaza, a place ruled by the local version of the Moslem Brotherhood (not to mention the German Nazis) called Hamas.

But whereas Levine (assuming that his surname would silence anybody tempted to call him an antisemite) identified himself primarily as "a Leftist," Ehrenreich chose to identify himself and to write (in that by now risible locution) primarily *as a Jew*, who had been taught (by Marxist grandparents, to be sure) and still believes in a kindergarten version of Jewish history usually called *Leidensgeschichte* ("suffering history"). Like many "progressive" Jews Ehrenreich has discovered that voting for Barack Obama and supporting homosexual marriage and abortion rights are not quite sufficient to sustain a Jewish identity: only anti-Zionism will do that. For no extra charge, he placed himself in the "prophetic tradition" of Jeremiah and Amos, having apparently forgotten that although these two did believe that the Babylonians and other miscreants acted as God's Cossacks in punishing Israel for its sins, they did not—as Ehrenreich, in the centuries-old manner of Jewish apostates, certainly does—set themselves apart from Jerusalem and identify with its enemies—just how fully would be revealed a few years later. (In assessing Ehrenreich's claim to descent from the Hebrew prophets, I leave aside the matter of literary power, in which realm he is much closer to Thomas Friedman than to Amos and Jeremiah.)

The *Times Magazine* spread portrays, with love, sympathy, and sycophancy, the villagers (without exception charming "people like you and me") of Nabi Saleh in the disputed territories who (so Ehrenreich hopes) will provide the manpower for the next intifada. (The last one, lest we forget, killed over a thousand Israelis and maimed ten times that number in acts of which animals would be ashamed.) The *Times*'s cover photos included at least two children among the budding heroes and heroines of the hoped for "Third Intifada." One of them, eleven-year-old Ahed Tamimi, had already been honored by Turkey's demagogic Jew-hating Prime Minister Erdogan (Barack Obama's "favorite European leader") for her much-photographed provocations of Israeli soldiers. Another member of the Tamimi family, Ahlan, remains (in Ehrenreich's treacly prose) "much loved in Nabi Saleh." And why? The parents of another child, Arnold and Frimet Roth, explain:

> That's all he [Ehrenreich] writes about Ahlan Tamimi but we can tell you more. She is a Jordanian who was 21 years old and the newsreader on official Palestinian Authority television when she signed on with Hamas to become a terrorist. She engineered, planned and helped execute a massacre in the center of Jerusalem on a hot summer afternoon in 2001. She chose the target, a restaurant filled with Jewish children. And she brought the bomb. The outcome (15 killed, a sixteenth still in a vegetative state today, 130 injured) was so uplifting to her that she has gone on camera again and again to say, smiling into the camera lens, how proud she is of what she did. She is entirely free of regret."[1]

This little detail about "much loved" Ahlan is missing from Ehrenreich's saints' tale. Also missing is a quotation of the *raison d'être* of Hamas, the organization that may already, in summer 2014, have begun Intifada Three, as stated in Article Seven of its founding covenant: "The Prophet, ... peace be upon him, says: 'The hour of judgment shall not come until the Muslims fight the Jews and kill them, so that the Jews hide behind trees and stones, and each tree and stone will say: "Oh Muslim, oh servant of Allah, there is a Jew behind me, come and kill him."'"[2]

The question that entered my mind when reading Ehenreich's adoring portrait of these trainees in "resistance" to the "occupation" was the following: "Couldn't something like this celebration of past and potential murderers of Jews have been published in the *Dearborn Independent*?" My first reply was "of course." This hateful paper, which was financed by Henry Ford from 1919 to 1927 and reached a circulation of 900,000 in 1925, has long been considered the most antisemitic of American newspapers. But my second reply was "no, not really—the *Dearborn Independent* stopped short of explicitly inciting murder of, or violence against, Jews." Moreover, its publisher Henry Ford in 1927 apologized, in an open letter to Louis Marshall of the American Jewish Committee, for "the wrong done to the Jews as fellow-men and brothers" by his paper, and asked "their forgiveness for the harm that I have unintentionally committed."[3] Will the Sulzberger family ever do the same? Probably not—for *NY Times* editors know no limits where the "Palestinian" issue is concerned. For them the dividing line between moral and immoral, permitted and forbidden, is like the receding horizon; they keep moving toward it, but can never quite reach it.

A year after Ehrenreich's celebration of murderers past and future, in June 2014, a fierce controversy erupted over New York's Metropolitan Opera plan to perform (and disseminate in hundreds of movie theaters) an operatic production called "The Death of Klinghoffer." The opera (originally performed years earlier in England) depicts the murder of an aging and disabled American Jew, Leon Klinghoffer, by Palestinian Arab terrorists during their 1985 hijacking of the Italian cruise ship *Achille Lauro.* Klinghoffer was shot in the head and chest and then, still in his wheelchair, shoved into the sea. The libretto, composed by an American Jewish convert to the Church of England (in which she now serves as a parish priest), sympathetically portrays the killers and their apologia (*not* apology) for murder.

The *Times* editorial board, on June 20, endorsed the opera, deplored the cancellation of the scheduled simulcasts, and urged the Met to resist pressure by Jewish groups to cancel the eight performances still scheduled for live production at the Met. It further suggested that the opera be accompanied (precisely as the murderers and their adoring followers wished) by public discussions about "the Middle East conflict." (No doubt the *Times* would, for a suitable fee, offer its resident experts on the subject—Thomas Friedman or Jodi Rudoren—as moderators.)

One might have thought that a paper so concerned with its own history and the need for repair of an institutional reputation badly tarnished by its deliberate obfuscation of the dimensions of Germany's war against European Jewry[4] would be more cautious about giving free rein to the untidy passions of its Jewish Israel-haters and their friends. But no: the motto on the Sulzberger family's coat of arms appears to be: UNASHAMED. So important to the paper is the goal of converting those Jews who still, in the words of Elijah on Mt. Carmel, "halt between two opinions," and bringing them to the side of Baal.

One can only hope that this overzealousness at the *Times* has served to remind at least some of its Jewish readers of a truth that Saul Bellow stated in 1976: "There is one fact of Jewish life unchanged by the creation of a Jewish state: you cannot take your right to live for granted. Others can; you cannot. . . . The Jews, because they are Jews, have never been able to take the right to live as a natural right."[5]

Notes

1. See "Simply Adorable Kids of the Third Intifada—Cute and Cuddly," *Jerusalem Post*, March 23, 2013.

2. Also killed in the Sbarro bombing was an Israeli teenager named Malki Roth. Some time before being murdered by Ehrenreich's "much loved" Ahlan Tamimi, she had addressed a Rosh Hashanah letter to God expressing the hope that she would live another year, and that the Messiah would arrive. This so infuriated the Anglo-Jewish Israel hater Jacqueline Rose that, in the course of one of her countless apologias for mass murderers as "people driven to extremes," she rhapsodized about bonding with Islamist fanatics, lashed out against "those wishing to denigrate suicide bombers and their culture," and insisted that that "culture" is superior to the Jewish culture of the butchered Malki Roth. Rose, a psychoanalytic literary critic, helps one to understand why enemies of psychoanalysis sometimes disparage it as being the disease it purports to cure.

3. See *Statement by Henry Ford: Regarding Charges Against Jews Made in His Publications, The Dearborn Independent, and a Series of Pamphlets Entitled 'The International Jew,' Together With an Explanatory Statement by Louis Marshall, President of The American Jewish Committee, and His Reply to Mr. Ford* (New York: The American Jewish Committee, 1927.

4. See the books on this subject by Deborah Lipstadt (*Beyond Belief: The American Press & the Coming of the Holocaust: 1933–1945* (New York: The Free Press, 1986) and Laurel Leff, *Buried By the Times: The Holocaust and America's Most Important Newspaper* (New York: Cambridge University Press, 2006).

5. Saul Bellow, *To Jerusalem and Back* (New York: Viking, 1976), 26.

Selected Bibliography

Auerbach, Jerold. http://www.algemeiner.com/2014/12/21/hannukah-greet-
    ings-from-the-new-york-times
    _____http://www.americanthinker.com/articles/2015/01/the_politics_of_
    dead_children_.html
Bogdanor, Vernon. "History Lessons." *Jewish Chronicle*, January 29, 1993.
Brahm, Gabriel and Cary Nelson, *The Case Against Academic Boycotts of
    Israel*. Detroit: Wayne State University Press, 2014.
Halkin, Hillel. *Letters to an American-Jewish Friend: A Zionist's Polemic*
    (Philadelphia: Jewish Publication Society, 1977.
Joffe, Alex. http://spme.org/boycotts-divestments-sanctions-bds/bds-
    academia-politics-industry-spme-bds-monitor/16778/#.Uu8auuEYXBo.
    email
    _____http://www.algemeiner.com/2015/01/01/on-college-campuses-
    semester-ends-with-big-bds-push/
Karsh, Efraim. "Running Away from Statehood." http://besacenter.org/
    perspectives-papers/running-away-statehood/?utm_source=rss&utm_
    medium=rss&utm_campaign=running-away-statehood
Kramer, Martin. "The American Studies Association's Next Boycott." http://
    www.commentarymagazine.com/2014/01/07/the-asas-next-boycott/
Marks, Jonathan. https://www.commentarymagazine.com/2014/10/06/the-
    judaism-of-self-congratulation/#.VDKd5PRl2J8.email
    _____http://chronicle.com/blogs/conversation/2014/05/21/zionist-attack-
    dogs-the-mlas-debate-on-israel-might-go-viral/
Merlin, Samuel. *Millions of Jews to Rescue: A Bergson Group Leader's Account
    of the Campaign to Save Jews from the Holocaust*, ed. Rafael Medoff. Wash-
    ington, D. C.: Wyman Institute, 2011.
Muravchik, Joshua. *Making David into Goliath: How the World Turned against
    Israel*. San Francisco: Encounter Books, 2014.
Nirenberg, David. *Anti-Judaism: The Western Tradition*. New York and
    London: W. W. Norton, 2013.
Steyn, Mark, http://www.ruthfullyyours.com/2015/01/20/a-judenrein-jew-
    cleansed-europe-mark-steyn/
Tobin, Jonathan. https://www.commentarymagazine.com/2013/03/12/why-
    debate-the-jewish-state-prejudice/#.UT-1tF8aMpE.email

Index

153